FINDsomeone.com

FINDsomeone.com

R. Scott Grasser

Butterworth–Heinemann

Boston Oxford Johannesburg Melbourne New Delhi Singapore

Library of Congress Cataloging-in-Publication Data
Grasser, R. Scott (Ralph Scott), 1961-
    FINDsomeone.com / R. Scott Grasser.
        p.   cm.
    Includes index.
    ISBN 0-7506-7020-7
    1. Missing persons—Investigation—United States—Handbooks,
    manuals, etc.   2. Public records—United States—Handbooks, manuals,
    etc.   I. Title.
    HV6762.U5G73   1998
    363.2'336—dc21   97-32403
                                                          CIP

British Library Cataloguing-in-Publication Data
A catalogue record for this book is available from the British Library.

The publisher offers special discounts on bulk orders of this book.
For information, please contact:
Manager of Special Sales
Butterworth–Heinemann
225 Wildwood Avenue
Woburn, MA 01801-2041
Tel: 781-904-2500
Fax: 781-904-2620

For information on all Butterworth-Heinemann publications available, contact our World Wide Web home page at: http://www.bh.com

10 9 8 7 6 5 4 3 2 1

Printed in the United States of America

A rose of any splendor is no more magnificent than the gracefulness of the best rose: Hetta Rose Grasser.
And to America's best professional, silent, and secret warriors: The Green Berets.

Contents

Preface

This book is designed to provide simple investigative resources used by professionals today to locate people—under almost all circumstances. This book offers highly effective, proven techniques for conducting telephone searches, making use of government records, and accessing on-line information brokers. Core strategies for conducting genealogical searches and adoption investigations—for both birth parents and adopted children—are discussed in understandable terms in Chapters 6 and 7.

One of my students recently wrote to me after taking my *America Online* course, "Private Investigator Techniques," expressing appreciation for the techniques she had learned. "I took your class in hopes of finding my daughter," she wrote. "I wanted to thank you for rekindling my hopes and for the ultimate success I had in finding her. Not only did I find a daughter—but a son-in-law and three grandchildren! I'm 45 and have no other children, so I can't begin to tell you what all this means to me."

With this book, you have access to these same techniques. Take a moment to glance down the chapter titles in the table of contents. Nothing available today offers better, more up-to-date guidance in finding missing persons than does this book.

About the Author

R. Scott Grasser is an international security consultant and licensed private investigator, with both corporate and governmental experience and a background in leadership training and military intelligence. As a Captain in the U.S. Army, Grasser was assigned to Special Forces command, investigating hundreds of criminal, counter-intelligence, security, and surveillance cases. Grasser has also competed in and finished the Canadian Armed Forces Iron Man Competition.

This book was prepared with editorial assistance from W. C. Selover, a freelance editor, journalist, and speech writer, and a former senior civilian public affairs official at the Pentagon. Selover is the principal of Chaparral Working Group, a communications consortium in San Francisco.

Introduction

The techniques I will share with you were developed over my many years in military intelligence and security and as a professional investigator. I have also made them available as a motivational speaker and as a teacher of courses offered by community organizations and by *America Online*. With this book, I am pleased to make these simple tools more widely available.

I have been asked why I would be willing to share some of my profession's most carefully protected secrets. That's simple. I have learned that in this increasingly mobile society—where neighbors are often strangers, and hometown roots and even families are distant and separated—there remains a deep longing to renew those earlier connections. Who hasn't considered attending a high school or college reunion? And who hasn't had a deep desire to see or learn about certain special people from their past? How often do the daytime talk shows focus on reunions with former sweethearts, estranged family members, or comrades from the armed services? Pretty often, it seems to me. That's because people feel a natural desire and curiosity to renew cherished, or sometimes painful, memories of the past—a desire that often can only be satisfied by the use of techniques perfected by professional private investigators. So let's start now and get you on your way to your own personal research adventure.

My first professional search case involved a woman who was seeking her cousin, a cousin not seen or heard from for forty-some-odd years. By using just my telephone, I was able to reunite the two the following weekend, even though a national search firm had tried for more than a year with no results. In less than an hour, I had found the missing person and the family was reunited. This was no miracle. I just applied the systematic methods and techniques described in this book, and I believe you too can achieve similar results—as my students have consistently proven.

There is no mystery to the professional methods used by private investigators and researchers nationwide. Many of my students have been able to find missing loved ones and friends by working hard at applying these techniques. In this book, I will discuss search theory, techniques, methods, and analysis for anticipating probable success in applying various search products. And I will describe where to find professional, qualified information brokers. With thousands of private commercial and governmental data banks available today, well over 90 percent of Americans may be located by the methods described here. Most importantly, you can do it yourself.

There is a truism in the intelligence field that "everything can be found out—it only takes time and money." In this book, I hope to demonstrate methods and techniques that can, within a short period of time, reunite you with your loved ones, allow you to find missing friends, and *save you money at the same time.*

WHY ARE PEOPLE MISSING?

It's usually easy to determine why people are missing. Generally, there are two types of missing persons cases. The first is the person who is really not missing but has simply lost touch with friends, family, and classmates. They probably don't even know anyone is looking for them. They might even be an unknowing beneficiary of an estate. The second is the person who has engaged in some type of illegal activity or owes money, and they simply to do not want to face the consequences of their actions. Most often this second case involves someone deliberately skipping out on a loan or payment of some sort. Or it could be an unwilling witness to a crime who doesn't want to get involved. When searching for persons in either case, the investigative techniques are identical. In this field, *a case is a case is a case!*

After having located a particularly elusive witness, I am occasionally asked by an attorney, "How in the world did you find this person?" My reply is always the same: "To know *that* . . . costs extra!!" But actually finding missing witnesses is really fairly simple, so here are the secrets that private investigators use:

Before beginning a case, I always carefully determine the answers to two basic questions:

- First, what is the goal of the investigation? Goals are like road maps, and you need to know at the outset where you are headed and when the destination has been reached.
- The second covers equally important territory: what information is known or can be obtained right away? Ask yourself, can I readily acquire an address of the individual being sought that is seven years old or less? A full, correct name? An accurate social security number? The date and place of birth? Obviously, knowing the answers to these questions will help determine what additional information will need to be developed.

The goal of almost all missing witness cases is to discover the subject's full and correct name, home or work address, and home or work telephone number, or some way to communicate with the witness in writing or by telephone.

I have found that an investigation can best be developed as a "human interest story," using a human intelligence (HUMINT) source to provide at least the bare outlines of the story. The initial story can be verified for accuracy, and an outside source may then be identified to provide updated or more known information. This outside source of information can be a manual search of county records located within the county clerk's office, recorder's office, tax assessor's office, or court records, and maybe all of these. An outside source also may be an on-line search of a subject's social security number (SSN), whether you or an information broker conducts the search.

The investigation then continues by evaluating the new outside-source information. On occasion, when such information yields little or no additional elements to the story, we continue to check other outside sources until we find some leads or until our investigative goal is reached. The evaluation phase might suggest a return to human collection of information or possibly a continuation of the on-line search. Once we have gathered definitive information—for example, the updated address of the subject—we then complete the investigation by verifying this new information. If all goes well, and the subject of the investigation is located and verified, then our investigation is over. If not, then we systematically continue to explore new leads and verify the information until the cycle is complete and the desired goals are achieved.

An investigation relies on the gathering of known information on the subject, recorded on a worksheet referred to as the "dossier." Information including the subject's name, last known address, employment, and telephone numbers are listed as reference points. These factors represent nonchanging subject identification information. Store the accumulated information in the dossier folder and organize it carefully for access later.

But before moving to the sample dossier, I want to first introduce you to one of the most effective on-line search products available for developing credible information on your subject. It's called a "credit header." A credit header is simply the name, address, social security number, and sometimes the telephone number of an individual that appears at the beginning of a credit report. The credit header itself does not provide financial account information—*that* is called a credit report—but it lists crucial identifying information on an individual. Credit headers generally will produce information on someone within a time frame going back seven years. Information older than that might not show up on the report. Nonetheless, its value is obvious. As a person moves and changes addresses, credit card and loan information follows an individual. In our society, having access to credit is critical, and if someone does not pay bills on time, their access to credit is jeopardized. Even if someone has a bad credit, an individual might try to reestablish credit someplace else, in another state. One of the keys to this type of search is repeating it again after a few months, since individuals often attempt to reestablish credit. So the credit header is a significant search product, and its access will be described in detail later.

A word of caution: in order to run a trace utilizing a name, the full name is essential. Quite often the full and accurate name of the subject is not initially available. Most often a nickname—such as Bob or Ray—is given as a first name. Of course, Robert or Raymond is the legal name to look for on reports or traces. Often, however, such nicknames refer to middle names of the subject, or not to any given name at all, and thus will not provide a match in standard tracing procedures. Additionally, of course, a woman's last name is likely to change over time through marriage and divorce. In cases where the middle or last name is the variable, the known quantity is often the last-known employment or last-known address of the subject. Then you can work backward, and the credit header will provide the full name. Middle initials, spouse's name, or place of employment information can often be uncovered on the credit header report.

A comprehensive listing of all the information we will need may include: all previous addresses and telephone numbers, beginning with the most recent ones and moving back to former ones; adoption information; age of the individual; birth date and place; burial location; death information, such as date and place (as applicable); hobbies; marital status, marriage records, and information of possible previous marriages; employment; ethnic background; immigration records; maiden name; name and place of employment of spouse; names of children; names of living relatives together with addresses, telephone numbers, and places of employment; naturalization records; previous research about the individual; religion or church membership; social security number; and U.S. military service records—to name a few.

To retrieve this nonchanging positive identification information, one can go to a number of different sources. For example, if you are looking for someone who is still alive, then the most recent information is the best, and then you can go backward as necessary. If you are searching for someone who is deceased, for genealogical purposes, then the researcher would want to continue to accumulate historical information, not stopping until this leads to other identified family members.

Sources of information with which to begin a search are obvious, such as old letters, neighbors, school yearbooks, other research, and even trash can be a good source. This method is commonly called a "dumpster dive" by professional private investigators. Getting someone's discarded trash is often a gold mine of information. This includes old envelopes, personal notes, or letters. Habits to notice include cigarette, alcohol, and eating habits, which tell a lot about a person. For example, the discovery of health food containers means we probably will not find our subject at a fast-food restaurant. Remember, if you use this method, wear industrial-strength rubber gloves!

A listing of the subject's known characteristics can be assembled using the prototype dossier in Form 1. Begin with the subject's nonchanging specifics. Information on this form is listed in order of importance. When beginning a search, fill out this form for each subject being researched. The bulleted point represents suggested actions to be taken to locate this individual.

	Fill in responses here
Legal and Proper Name (full first, middle, and last) • possible surname search • possible "Super Search" product	
Height, weight, color of hair, color eyes, family information, etc.	
Last and all known Telephone Numbers • possible crisscross search	
Social Security number • possible credit "header" search	
All Addresses (current or last known) • possible address update on-line search if within the last seven years • "Super Search" product	
Current and all known Employment (name, address, and telephone number) • possible telephone call to human resource department	
Driver's License or Automobile License • possible on-line DMV search by state	
Relatives/Friends • possible telephone call as long-lost friend	
Schools (start with most recently attended) • possible telephone call to alumni association or admissions department	
Business Connections • on-line business search, numerous products	
State Professional Licenses • on-line search/telephone call to the state's licensing bureau	
Former or Current Military • possible contact with U.S. Government	
Credit Information • only with subject's approval or when legal, consult attorney	
Association Memberships • possible telephone to association	
Date of Birth • possible check of county criminal information or drivers check by state	

FORM 1   Subject Dossier (Fill out a separate form for each subject.)

Chapter 1

Telephone Use and Pretexting—
Your Most Powerful Tool!

When searching for missing persons, the telephone is your most important tool. The telephone is to a researcher what a camera is to a photographer. Without the telephone, the researcher is out of business. This tool offers immediate, direct contact with an expert—commonly known as a human intelligence [HUMINT] source.

But how do you get this information source to be forthcoming? Here, it is crucial that you develop a credible message that will evoke help from the authorities—providing them with the motivation to share information.

How to do this? Two basic approaches are used: the first is the *Plain Truth* (i.e., "I am a friend of the subject and am looking for him since we have not spoken since school"); the second approach is called *Pretexting*. The plain truth is easy to understand, but what about pretexting? Some call it *pretending*—and, admittedly, that pretty much says it. Pretexting is the development of a story designed to motivate an expert to provide the information necessary to locate the individual. In the investigative business, potential sources can either be sympathetic to our efforts, or not. By relying on a courteous approach, thoughtful questions, and employing some degree of natural charm, our goal here is to create a comfortable situation where our source will not be placed on the defensive. Remember, this expert is rarely required to talk with us, so to ingratiate ourselves we will need to put on our best face. To do this takes practice. And it also takes a *stratagem*, or a ruse.

THE STRATAGEM

Using your imagination, anticipate and plan for the conversation. Ensure that your story is credible. Ask yourself, why would someone be calling and asking for information? The most believable story is the obvious one: you are tracking down a long-lost friend from college, updating alumni information, or organizing a reunion. Or you are calling from a company verifying employment information prior to hiring, and so on. Is this legal? As long as you do not pretext as a known company when, in fact, you are not conducting that company's business, you are on pretty safe grounds.

Practice what you are going say, and practice being a professional—as if you routinely verify information on people for a living. Be yourself and attempt to put the other person at ease. Remember, the expert is working at a job like most of us and is most likely just interested in doing a good job. After you are comfortable with your pretext, consider first calling the individual or expert who knows the most. Make the calls, and write down all the results on the dossier sheet form provided. Your search is then launched. Your first conversation might go something like this.

Subject: Susan B. James

Expert:	"Hello, ABC Corporation."
You:	"Human resources, please."
Expert:	"Human resources, Mike speaking."
You:	"Hi Mike, this is John Smith, and I am verifying employment for Susan B. James. (Ask the question first, seizing the initiative. Don't give the expert time to consider whether they are going to help you or not; give them a mission in a nice way.) Is Susan B. James currently employed at ABC corporation, and in what capacity?"
Expert:	"Who are you?"
You:	"Mike, I am John Smith, and I am verifying employment records (or for Keyboard Financial). I'm sorry to trouble you, but, unfortunately, this report is late, and I really would like to try to wrap up this assignment today. I have been out sick for a week."
Expert:	"Well, hold on, I will check."
You:	"Thank you."
Expert:	"Susan B. James is no longer an employee at ABC Corporation."
You:	"I wonder if you would be able to tell me her dates of employment and capacity and the amount of compensation?"
Expert:	"Well, let's see. Susan James worked at ABC Corporation from October 1995 until September of 1996 as a file clerk at $2,100.00 a month."
You:	"Thank you very much. Oh, by the way can you tell me if she is currently employed and where?" (Always ask a follow-up question for additional information.)
Expert:	"Well, I believe she left here and went to BCD Corporation."
You:	"Thank you very much and have a good day."

Remember, don't record these conversations, since it is generally illegal without two-party consent. Don't spoil a good operation by violating any law.

THE RULES FOR PRETEXTING

The general rules here are to *ask bright, clear, and concise questions*. Concise questions provide easily understandable information in the same sentence that ends with a question. It gives the expert enough information to volunteer further information that is then helpful to us. If we don't bring some information to the table, our expert might become defensive and unwilling to divulge critical information. Clear questions, of course, truly *ask the question*. In other words, ask and ye shall receive an answer! But you must actually ask the question, or the listener will not clearly understand that he or she is expected to respond. In all the examples in this section, the listener is expected to volunteer information. And the expert does so because we have provided enough background information to enlist them in our cause.

What you should *not* do is ask obscure questions no one can understand or attempt to throw your weight around. Being domineering and pushy will get us nothing—except someone on the other end of the telephone hanging up. If someone says they don't feel comfortable talking with you, thank them immediately and acknowledge their concerns, but then ask just one more question prior to hanging up. But always be polite (the world has enough aggressive telephone cranks). For example, a conversation where someone becomes defensive might be handled in the following way.

THE EMPLOYMENT VERIFICATION STRATEGY

Expert: "Hello."

You: "Hi! Human Resources please."

Expert: "Can I help you?"

You: "I need to verify employment of Mary Chen."

Expert: "We don't do that."

You: "Is there anyone there that could help me?"

Expert: "No."

You: "Do you verify employment of former employees?"

Expert: "No, it is policy that we do not."

You: "Okay, thank you. Oh, by the way, where did Mary Chen work?"

Expert: "I'm not sure. Accounting Department, I think."

You: "Thank you."

New call. Same case.

Expert: "Hello."

You: "Accounting Department, please."

Expert: "This is Accounting."

You:	"Hi, I'm verifying Mary Chen's employment there. Does anyone remember her working there?"
Expert:	"Yes I do, she worked with me for two years."
You:	"Can you tell me if she is re-hirable there?"
Expert:	"Oh, you must talk to HR."
You:	"Yes, I have spoken to HR, and they told me to call Accounting, since she worked there."
Expert:	"Okay, yes, she worked here for two years, and held the position of accounting clerk."
You:	"Not manager?" [She told someone she was the manager!]
Expert:	"No. Just a clerk."
You:	"Thank you very much. Oh, by the way, could you tell me if she left voluntarily or involuntarily?"
Expert:	"She did not leave voluntarily."
You:	"Do you know if she was able to obtain new employment?"
Expert:	"I think at a temp agency."
You:	"Do you know which one?"
Expert:	"Maybe Kelly's Secretaries."
You:	"Okay. Thank you."

Now call Kelly's Secretaries, after obtaining the number from the telephone book or from an on-line directory. What we are doing here is creating an innocent subterfuge.

Once you get into the calling mode, stay with it! You are now into the swing of this. Go ahead and call other leads or sources. I recommend never taking a break at this point.

THE ALUMNI STRATAGEM

Subject: Mark Burton

This time you are calling Union University Alumni Department. (The alumni department at *my* college always seems to be able to track me down to ask for money!) Here's how this stratagem might go:

Expert:	"Hello."
You:	"Hello, may I speak with someone in the alumni association that handles mailings?"
Expert:	"Yes, I can help you."

You: "Hi, this is James Detrich, and I am planning a high school reunion for Garden Grove High School. However, I have lost contact with Mark Burton. I believe he graduated in 1991or some time around then."

Expert: "Well, okay. Wait a minute."

You: "Thank you."

Expert: "Mark Burton graduated in 1993, and we have him listed at 2301 West Fourth Street, San Francisco, CA 94118. Do you need his telephone number?"

You: "Oh sure, please."

Expert: "That number is 415-555-1234."

You: "Thank you very much, and have a nice day."

This can get more complicated, but with practice your imagination will flower. And getting good at this requires nothing less than practice and preparation. Remember, too, always be relaxed.

THE GENEALOGY STRATAGEM

Another example is calling a neighbor or former employer.

Subject: Harry K. Furman

Expert: "Hello."

You: "Hi. This is Mary Cassell with ABC Genealogy Service, and we are looking to put together lost members of the Furman family. We know the Furman family settled in New York in the late 1800s, yet members of the family moved soon after that. I understand a Furman family lived next to you recently but have moved. Is that correct?"

Expert: "Yes. That was about six months ago."

You: "Can you tell me how we can contact this family?"

Expert: "No, but I know they moved to Los Angeles."

You: "Would you know where Mr. or Mrs. Furman work?"

Expert: "He was an attorney."

You: "Thank you, and have a good day."

THE UNCLAIMED CHECK OR UNCLAIMED PROPERTY STRATAGEM

Here's another example: the *unclaimed check or unclaimed property stratagem.* Here we use pretexting as a follow-up to an on-line neighborhood search (approximately $15 or so) that has provided us with Jim Smith's neighbors. This search results in a list of names and telephone numbers, based on address Data Entry surrounding the address requested. The results might look something like this:

Search address: 2391 Union Street, San Francisco, California 94109
Search results: 10 addresses searched

2388 Union Street, James Jones, 857-0091

2389 Union Street, Sam Lickman, 564-3439

2392 Union Street, Mary Casie, 983-8305

2393 Union Street, Heck Mansfred, 925-7438

2394 Union Street, Del Smyth, 873-8734

2397 Union Street, Jui Chun, 983-3498

2398 Union Street, Chi Jung, 983-3983

2399 Union Street, San Hue, 393-3433

2400 Union Street, Jane Kilgore, 298-3498

2401 Union Street, Holt Cassell, 230-3349

This search can best be employed if the subject has moved away from 2391 Union Street only within the last few years. With this list in hand, we begin calling neighbors of the missing person, starting with the neighbors right next door. For example, Heck Mansfred at 415-925-7438, living at 2393 Union Street.

The conversation might go something like this:

Expert: "Hello."

You: "May I speak with Mr. Heck Mansfred?"

Expert: "This is Heck Mansfred."

You: "Mr. Mansfred, I am Sally Jones at Decisive Financial Group, and I am attempting to settle an old claim with one of your former neighbors, Mr. Jim Smith. Our records show that Mr. Smith's claim check has been returned, and I have no information updating Mr. Smith's present address. Could you help me?"

Expert: "The post office should have the address. I am sure his mail is being forwarded."

You: "Unfortunately, the address-forward period has expired, and his mail is being returned to our check department."

Expert: "Well, I don't know if I can help. Jim and his family moved away over a year ago, and I don't know the present address."

You: "Do you know what city and state Mr. Smith has moved to?"

Expert: "Yes, he moved to Dallas, Texas, for a new job. I remember his wife was from Texas, and she seemed happy to be moving back."

You: "Thank you very much, and have a good day."

Now, after the pretext has limited our subject's location to Dallas, Texas, we can start using telephone directories for the search. Some directories are free and updated every six months or so and are found on the World Wide Web. Another technique is to call 214-555-1212, the telephone company's information operator, to find even more updated information. If the telephone directories prove useless, then alpha name searches throughout Texas can be used, with full proper first name of "James" and the last name, for more possible information. I will discuss such searches in greater detail in Chapter 4, which explores ways of using pretext techniques that rely on other information leads.

Some of the most common places to call:

1. Former or current employers, including boss, Human Resources, or, even better, coworkers (you can sometimes get employer information from a "credit header")
2. Former or current school's alumni associations or registrar's offices
3. Family members
4. Neighbors or former neighbors
5. Friends
6. Associations or clubs
7. Hangouts (bars, restaurants, etc.)

Some of the most common places *not* to call:

1. The telephone company, unless all you want is published information. (But you can get a copy of your spouse's cell phone calls here!)
2. Utility companies. By law, they cannot give out information, unless it is for yourself.
3. Attorneys

Chapter 2

The Manual Search of Government Records: County, State, and Federal

Although a great deal is written elsewhere about searching government records, I felt I should include this chapter for the sake of providing a thorough reference resource. Government public records in general are easy to understand. First and foremost they are public. The taxpayers own them! That's right, they belong to all of us. So you have legitimate access to them. Only when such records are specifically designated confidential, as in personnel records of employees, for example, or those dealing with national security, does the government conceal records. So what records are available, and where do I find them?

CITY AND COUNTY LEVEL

The greatest source of information is found at the city and county levels. Although they include over eighty-five types of records, here are the ones most commonly used, most of which are accessed through computer-based terminals within the city and county offices.

These records are located at city and county offices. In larger cities, some records are maintained under the aegis of the city government and some under county jurisdiction, depending on the nature of the political subdivision. However, I suggest that you visit nearby offices—drawn from those listed below—for a thorough education as to the content of these records and to discover how easy they are to acquire.

In later chapters, I will discuss some of the on-line computer records available through information brokers, but the actual hard-copy files residing in the county offices (even at state and federal level offices) are more complete and provide more information than can an on-line computer search. The reason is that computer on-line searches uncover reports that are often summaries of the actual files. Naturally, then, record files are going to have more detailed information. Professionals are thoroughly familiar with these records, and they are authorities at accessing them—which is why they charge for their services. No doubt, these records and their acquisition are complicated. Simply put, there are too many offices and too many counties! But once you have experience in using the

TABLE 2.1   City and County Level

Type of General File To Be Found	Level of Access You Might Find or Restrictions
(Remember, each city and county government has different levels of allowable access, reflected only broadly in this general table.)	
Assignments (lien, judgment, etc.)	Access generally no problem
Birth	Access generally no problem, cross references available sometimes by date or name
Business license (city level)	Access generally no problem
Criminal case filings and complete court records	Access generally no problem (must have case number, which can sometimes be found at municipal or superior court filing offices, then go to the records room for the actual file)
Civil litigation case filings and complete court records	Access generally no problem (must have case number, which can sometimes be found at municipal or superior court filing offices, then go to the records room for the actual file)
Death	Access generally no problem
Deeds (county recorder's office)	Access generally no problem
Easement	Access generally no problem
Fictitious business names	Access generally no problem
Marriage	Access generally no problem
Pet, hunting, and fishing licenses (city level)	Local laws apply
Power of attorneys	Access generally no problem
Property ownership (county recorder's office, and can be cross checked by tax assessor's office)	Access generally no problem
Probate court filings and complete court records	Access generally no problem
Marriage, separation, and divorce	Access generally no problem
Small claims court	Access generally no problem (must have case number, which can sometimes be found at municipal or superior court filing offices, then go to the records room for the actual file)
Tax assessment and payment	Access generally no problem
Voter's registration	Sometimes restricted for political purposes only, but will provide name, address, telephone number, oftentimes occupation, and additional information—this is the record a lot of professional PI's use

base files and documents, the on-line computer searches make more sense, and you will then more clearly understand the limitations of such searches.

STATE RECORDS

State records represent an outstanding resource, and they are the only source of comprehensive, statewide research information. Some of the state information is available directly from state offices. However, because I want you to be able to solve research cases within hours, let me describe the practical access you may have to these records.

TABLE 2.2   State Level

Type of General File To Be Found	Level of Access You Might Find or Restrictions
(Remember, again, each state government has varying levels of allowable access, but this table reflects general practice.)	
Birth	Some restrictions apply; generally approval of parties is needed
Business license	Access generally no problem
Criminal case filings and complete court records	Access generally no problem (again, must have case number, which can sometimes be found at municipal or superior court filing offices, then go to the records room for the actual file)
Civil litigation case filings and complete court records	Access generally no problem (must have case number, which can sometimes be found at municipal or superior court filing offices, then go to the records room for the actual file)
Death	Access generally no problem
Department of Motor Vehicles (DMV)	Access generally restricted (some states have few or no limitations)
Divorce	Some restrictions apply
Fictitious business names	Access generally no problem
Marriage	Some restrictions apply
Professional licensing	Access generally no problem
Tax, business (only, no personal records)	Access generally no problem
Uniform Commercial Code (UCC)	Access generally no problem (provides associations to business activity by name)
University or colleges	Some restrictions

TABLE 2.3   U.S. Government Level

Type of General File To Be Found	Level of Access You Might Find or Restrictions
Bankruptcy (Federal court level)	Access generally no problem
Criminal case filings and complete court records (Federal court level)	Access generally no problem (must have case number)
Civil litigation case filings and complete court records (Federal court level)	Access generally no problem (must have case number)
Social Security Administration	1-800-772-1213, will confirm if individual is living or dead and will forward a letter (you must have the social security number)
Inmate Locator Line	Public Information, Bureau of Prisons, U.S. Department of Justice, 320 1st St., NW, Room 64, Washington, DC 20536, (202) 307-3198, or the hotline at (202) 307-3126
U.S. Army Active Personnel Locator	U.S. Department of the Army, Worldwide Locator, EREC, Ft. Benjamin Harrison, IN 46249-5301, (317) 542-4211 (limited service provided)
Bureau of Naval Personnel	Navy Department, Washington, DC 20370 (limited service provided)
U.S. Marine Corps	Headquarters, Washington, DC 20380 (limited service provided)
U.S. Air Force	Airmen Records Annex, Randolph Air Force Base, San Antonio, TX 78291 (limited service provided)
U.S. Department of Transportation	U.S. Coast Guard, 400 7th Street SW, Washington, DC 20590 (limited service provided)
Army Discharged Personnel Locator Service	National Personnel Records Center, 9700 Page Blvd., St. Louis, MO 63132-5200, (314) 538-4201 (limited service provided)
Army Personnel Locator	U.S. Army Worldwide Locator, ELREC, Fort Benjamin Harrison, IN 46249-5301, (317) 542-4211 (limited service provided)
Military Records	National Personnel Records Center, Military Personnel Records, 9700 Page Avenue, St. Louis, MO 62132-5100, or E-mail at center@stlouis.nara.gov
Army Reserve Personnel Center	U.S. Department of the Army, 9700 Page Blvd., St. Louis, MO 63132-5200, (314) 538-3828 (limited service provided)

Once again, this is not a complete listing of information, but it is a compilation of the most often used and discussed records. I don't want to burden you with a compendium of all the records, but I do want you to become an expert on the common records. At the state level, records are generally more restricted than at local government offices. Why is this? Simply because state governments generally place greater control over records as they go from file to compilation form. In other words, access to a list of everything is more limited than is access to a single file (even though the file provides more information).

U.S. GOVERNMENT RECORDS

The key phrase here is "Freedom of Information Act." While these federal records are somewhat interesting and provide some military and other records, access takes time. A long wait is often the rule. Court records are available by going into the federal court-houses directly.

Chapter 3

World Wide Web On-Line Resources

The Internet is a remarkable resource. But it does have its limitations for use in researching and investigations. Most, if not all, of the records found on the Internet are public telephone numbers in directories. That means, simply, if someone does not want to be found, they just will not be listed in directories on the Internet. But for the Internet research that calls for seeking lost family, school mates, or friends, the Internet provides low-cost, national telephone directory access. The list below is not intended to be an exhaustive list of Internet sites but rather a simplified list of some of the more useful sites today. Since the Internet is considered mostly a "free" resource, the telephone and address directories are national white or yellow pages. I have not included sites that generally do not have databases. Nor have I attempted to include commercial sites that cannot produce interactive information that might be especially interesting to you or that do not provide some type of listing that can help you search better, such as a list of state genealogy libraries, for example.

TELEPHONE AND ADDRESS DIRECTORIES

These systems are based on telephone directories and loaded on electronic files, then loaded onto an Internet server. I sometimes use the Internet to start an investigation, just in case I "luck out" and find the subject listed with a published telephone number and address. However, I must say, I have yet to find anyone professionally on the Internet. Since most of my clients have already begun here, they all utilize data gathered by just three different information vendors: Database America, Metromail, and ProCD. These records are generally found to be three or more months out of date, but still represent a good place to begin. Remember that the telephone company's telephone directory, accessed by calling 411 or 555-1212, is generally one to two months out of date, and you must know the city in such cases.

Understand, of course, that if you are looking for a classmate or family member, these directories can prove useful, since most people in the United States move on average about every four years. So logic would suggest that if a directory is six months old, then the person might very well be still at the listed location and telephone number. Such directories—and there are hundreds of them—are based on one or two types of published information systems. In the next chapter we will talk about 5,000 data banks or more, held privately—based on tens of thousands of published information systems! A good starting place is at The Internet Sleuth, http://www.isleuth.com. This listing provides over 2,000 data banks at your fingertips. This site also has a reverse white pages directory that can start with just a telephone number, then tell you the ownership of the telephone number.

E-Mail Directories

- ESP E-MAIL SEARCH PROGRAM, http://www.esp.co.uk/
- FOUR11 DIRECTORY, http://www.four11.com
- HOUSERNET, http://www.housernet.com/ (search by demographics, not by name)
- INFOPLUS INTERNET DIRECTORY, http://www.infop.com/phone/isearch.html
- INTERNET, gopher://yaleinfo.yale.edu:7000/11/Internet_People
- INTERNET ADDRESS FINDER, http://www.iaf.net
- POPULUS, http://www.populus.net/

Toll-Free Directories

- AT&T 800 DIRECTORY, http://att.net/dir800/
- INTERNET 800 DIRECTORY, http://inter800.com/

White Pages or People-Finder Type Telephone Directories

- 411, http://www.411locate.com
- 555-1212, http://www.555-1212.com/ (includes E-mail)
- BIG FOOT, http://www.bigfoot.com/
- DATA BASE AMERICA, http://www.databaseamerica.com/
- FOUR11, http://www.four11.com
- INFOPLUS INTERNET DIRECTORY, http://www.infop.com/phone/isearch.html
- INFOSPACE, http://www.infospace.com/
- PC411, http://www.pc411.com/pc411.html
- PEOPLEFIND, http://www.lycos.com/pplfndr.html
- PEOPLE PAGE, http://www.peoplepage.com/index.html
- SWITCHBOARD, http://www.switchboard.com
- WHOWHERE? PHONE DIRECTORY, http://www.whowhere.com/phone.html
- YAHOO PEOPLE SEARCH, http://www.yahoo.com/search/people/

Yellow Pages Telephone Directories

- AMERICAN BUSINESS INFORMATION—LOOKUP, http://www.lookupusa.com/
- BIGBOOK, http://www.bigbook.com/
- BIGYELLOW, http://s16.bigyellow.com/

- GTE SUPER PAGES INTERACTIVE SERVICE, http://superpages.gte.com/
- ZIP2, http://www.zip2.com/
- NYNEX YELLOW PAGES, http://s14.bigyellow.com/
- ON VILLAGE YELLOW PAGES PLUS, http://www.onvillage.com/
- TRUE YELLOW, http://www.trueyellow.com/
- YELLOW NET WORLD WIDE PAGES, http://www.yellownet.com/
- YELLOW PAGES ON LINE, http://www.ypo.com/

- NASA, http://nic.nasa.gov/x500.html
- PAGENET WORLDWIDE MESSAGE CENTER,
  http://www.pagenet.net/pagenet/page_inp.htm
- CANADA 411, http://canada411.sympatico.ca

SOCIAL SECURITY NUMBER DEATH INDEXES

These data banks contain 75 million death records. (If you have a social security number, the Social Security Administration will give you the same information by calling 1-800-772-1213.)

- SOCIAL SECURITY NUMBER VALIDATION DATABASE,
  http://ourworld.compuserve.com/homepages/Task_Force/
- SOCIAL SECURITY DEATH INDEX, http://www.ancestry.com/ssdi
  Search by name or social security number.
  Returns: Birth date, date of death, and last residence.

FAA PILOT LICENSE AND AIRCRAFT REGISTRATION

- AIRCRAFT REGISTRATION DATABASE, http://www.via.net/test.html
  Features: No cost aircraft registration information, generally matches FAA registration database.
- LANDINGS, http://www1.drive.net/evird.acgi$pass*1661043!mtd*7!map*_landings/
  images/landings-strip.map?40,41
  Features: data bank on aircraft owners; alpha name search of U.S. registrations; certified pilots database; aviation medical examiners database; NTSB accident reports; and air worthiness directories.

OTHER INTERNET DATA BANK RESOURCES

- COPYRIGHT REGISTRATION SEARCH,
  gopher://marvel.loc.gov:70/11/copyright/research
- U.S. POSTAL SERVICE ZIP + 4,
  http://www.usps.gov/ncsc/lookups/lookup_zip+4.html
  Features: This is a nice free tool to verify if an address is real or not.

- DOCTOR SEARCH DATABASE, http://www.ama-assn.org/
  Features: AMA database, information on 650,000 doctors of all types.
- FLORIDA DEPARTMENT OF LAW ENFORCEMENT: SEXUAL PREDATORS
  DATABASE, http://www.fdle.state.fl.us
- YAHOO'S MAPS, http://maps.yahoo.com/yahoo
  Features: Point to point driving instructions.

GENEALOGY

- ANCESTRY'S SOCIAL SECURITY DEATH INDEX, http://www.ancestry.com/ssdi
- BEST GENEALOGY LINKS ON THE WWW,
  http://home.earthlink.net/~middleton/topten.html
- CYNDI'S GENEALOGY ON THE INTERNET,
  http://www.oz.net/~cyndihow/sites.htm (really a remarkable site with tons of infor-
  mation)
- CYNDI'S LIST OF VITAL RECORDS NATIONAL ADDRESSES,
  http://www.inlink.com/~nomi/vitalrec/staterec.html
- GENDEX, http://www.gendex.com/gendex/
- GENEALOGY GATEWAY, http://www.polaris.net/~legend/gateway5.htm
- GENEALOGY SF, http://www.genealogysf.com/gendatus.html
- GENEALOGY TOOLBOX, http://genealogy.tbox.com/
- GEANANET, http://www.geneanet.org/
- GERMAN GENEALOGY SOCIETY, http://www.genealogy.com/ (listed information)
- HELM'S GENEALOGY TOOLBOX,
  http://genealogy.tbox.com/query/wwwboard/index.html
- INTERNET SLEUTH, http://www.isleuth.com/gene.html
  (a super place to begin)
- OBITUARY DAILY TIMES, http://www.best.com/~shuntsbe/obituary/
- MORMANS or LDS, http://www.familyhistory.com/fhdata.htm
- NATIONAL ARCHIVES NAIL PROGRAM, http://www.nara.gov/nara/nail.html
- ROOTS SURNAME LIST, http://www.rootsweb.com/rootsweb/searches/
- ROOTSWEB, http://searches.rootsweb.com/cgi-bin/Genea/rsl
- SEVENTH DAY ADVENTIST OBITUARY LIST,
  http://143.207.5.3:82/screens/opacmenu.html
- U.S. CENSUS NAMES FREQUENCY,
  http://www.census.gov/genealogy/www/namesearch.html
- U.S. CENSUS POPULATION STATISTICS,
  http://www.census.gov/prod/www/subject.html
- U.S. GEN WEB, http://www.usgenweb.com/ (listings of compiled state-by-state ge-
  nealogy downloads)
- YAHOO!,
  http://www.yahoo.com/Arts/Humanities/History/Genealogy/Lineages_and_Surnames/
  and http://www.yahoo.com/Arts/Humanities/History/Genealogy

News groups represent an interesting and free method to elicit information by listing your search requests. I have included this list as one method to get the word out on your genealogy searches. This method is a *passive* investigative or research method, but nonetheless a good one. In the field of genealogy, you cannot be too timid in your methods. This simple but sometimes effective personal information marketing tool reaches hundreds of thousands of people. You can find these news groups with most Internet Service Providers (ISPs). Since it is free, I recommend using it, for you have nothing to lose and might gain the information desired. When posting a message here, make sure that your message is broad in topic, but specific in request. The topic of a family name like SMITH might produce too many E-mails or other postings; this leads to confusion. But a more specific request or posting might provide information better suited for this forum.

- Alt.genealogy at news:alt.genealogy
- soc.genealogy.african at news:soc.genealogy.african
- soc.genealogy.australia+nz at news:soc.genealogy.australia+nz
- soc.genealogy.benlux at news:soc.genealogy.benlux
- soc.genealogy.computing at news:soc.genealogy.computing
- soc.genealogy.french at news:soc.genealogy.french
- soc.genealogy.german at news:soc.genealogy.german
- soc.genealogy.hispanic at news:soc.genealogy.hispanic
- soc.genealogy.jewish at news:soc.genealogy.jewish
- soc.genealogy.medieval at news:soc.genealogy.medieval
- soc.genealogy.methods at news:soc.genealogy.methods
- soc.genealogy.misc at news:soc.genealogy.misc
- soc.genealogy.nordic at news:soc.genealogy.nordic
- soc.genealogy.slavic at news:soc.genealogy.slavic
- soc.genealogy.surnames at news:soc.genealogy.surnames
- soc.genealogy.uk+ireland at news:soc.genealogy.uk+ireland
- soc.roots at news:soc.roots

- LIBRARY OF CONGRESS, http://www.loc.gov
  Searchable index by author or keyword.
- OREGON SECRETARY OF STATE CORPORATION DIVISION UNIFORM COMMERCIAL CODE, http://www.sos.state.or.us/corporation/ucc/ucc.htm
  Searches Oregon state UCC filings; updated often.
- SECURITIES AND EXCHANGE COMMISSION FILINGS, http://www.sec.gov/
  SEC searches provide detailed information on companies that trade their stock on U.S. stock exchanges.
- RESEARCH-IT, http://www.iTools.com/research-it/research-it.html
  Research types: language, geographical, financial, Internet, shipping, and mailing.
- PAYPHONE COMPANIES, http://www.payphones.com/ipp.htm
- VETERANS ORGANIZATIONS AND VOLUNTEER LOCATOR, http://www.army.mil/vetinfo/vetloc.htm

FEDERAL GOVERNMENT WEB AND GOPHER LOCATIONS

I have included a list of Internet government data banks. Now these World Wide Web and gopher locations are great for research referrals, providing pathways to lists of locations that can assist in some researches. Most gopher files are download files not viewable on-line, but rather opened by applications off-line. By no means will these interactive data banks allow you to obtain personnel records or address updates, but they certainly should be listed here as a good reference resource.

- GENEALOGICAL RESOURCES ELSEWHERE ON THE INTERNET, http://gopher.nara.gov:70/1/
- GOVERNMENT INFORMATION EXCHANGE, http://www.info.gov/
- INFORMATION INFRASTRUCTURE TASK FORCE DOCUMENTS, INFORMATION AT DEPARTMENT OF COMMERCE—Not maintained by National Archives, http://iitf.doc.gov/
- INTERNATIONAL COUNCIL ON ARCHIVES (ICA), http://www.archives.ca/ica/
- LIBRARY OF CONGRESS (MARVEL), gopher://marvel.loc.gov/11/
- NATIONAL ARCHIVES GENEALOGY PAGE, http://www.nara.gov/genealogy
- U.S. GOVERNMENT MANUAL 1993/94, gopher://una.hh.lib.umich.edu/11/socsci/poliscilaw/govman

Chapter 4

Private On-Line Services

This chapter explores ways to go on-line with commercial data services. I will provide an overview of these services, a brief history of the industry, typical product pricing and products available, examples of an information broker's agreement, how you can establish a credit account with these services, and a directory of some on-line services. Some of these you can access by simply using your fax machine and credit card!

There are three things to remember about all on-line searches:

1. all on-line information was input by human beings,
2. so some information might be in error, and,
3. this on-line information cannot be disseminated in the form of input. It has been changed from a paper copy or magnetic tape file to a new electronic filing and storing system.

Thus, electronic, on-line information is available within the same corruption perimeters as is other forms of electronic media. The systems must have quality control from the beginning to the end of the collection process. This is why a high-quality and well-established information broker is invaluable.

A BRIEF HISTORY OF ON-LINE INFORMATION BROKERS

The history of this unusual information-broker industry goes back only a few years. Jack H. Reed of IRCS, Inc., contends that the information explosion began about 1982. Reed is a member of the Information Industry Association, the California Association of Licensed Investigators (CALI), and the National Counsel of Investigators and Security Services, and he has received numerous awards, including the CALI "distinguished achievement award." Reed also consults with the Federal Trade Commission and the White House Privacy Council, and on legislation regarding privacy and public records. When Reed asked why he was receiving his CALI award, a CALI member's response was that he had changed the face of the investigative industry. Indeed, he has. His company first provided extensive public records on-line to the business and investigation communities. Prior to this, individual county and state records were not massed in extensive data banks, making information acquisition difficult and only accessible at the local level—by going to the local government record offices.

In 1977, IBM announced its first release of a new and unknown machine, a computer called the PC. Few could anticipate the impact of this new, desktop-sized computer; in fact, many thought it not worthwhile. As a California-licensed investigator, Reed tells me that for two years he pondered the potential impact this small, compact machine could have on his business. Being an investigator since 1964 (and a very successful one at that), Reed knew the necessity of access to public records via electronic media. The old paper-file system was adequate, but time consuming. This entrepreneur wanted a faster and easier method to access billions of records nationally. At that time, investigators were considered merely regional operators, at best. By 1979, Reed was envisioning a rapid and inexpensive method of collecting, processing, storing, and transferring data. For those times, the concept was revolutionary. As Reed told me, "those seem like simple things now, but back then it was almost like witchcraft."

Believing that he might need a partner in this unfamiliar undertaking, Reed contacted a few California Association of Licensed Investigator members. The reaction he received time and time again was, "Jack, you're crazy." Not being easily dissuaded, Reed responded: "Well, I know that, but put that aside. Let's think of something logical. This looks like an opportunity, and I would rather partner it than do it myself." The response was a resounding, "Well, we'll think about it."

So while the other licensed private investigators were thinking about it, Reed bought an $18,000 IBM double-sided, dual-density, four-floppy-disk-drive, 610K-per-disk machine, and set out to put his PI business on computer. Reed was enormously proud of his new computer. Having experience as a credit card collection department manager, he knew a little about the Univac 1301 punch card computer. But this new PC was a horse of a different color. So Reed educated himself, first on how to spell "computer," then how to operate it, work a program, apply and make it function—all by working eighteen to twenty-hour days over many months. Learning some of the things to do and, just as important, the things *not* to do, Reed was ready for the next stage.

A computer consultant was hired and a 180-megabyte hard disk was bought to create the central server. They were ready for some real performance now. And when the first consultant left the company, another was hired—this time with excellent results. As Reed tells it, the first consultant could not keep up. "I was sort of ahead of the game, for I am known for my crazy ideas," he explained. "So I took the concept to another fellow who had some of the same crazy ideas, but he also knew a lot about computer hardware." So a company was formed called Debris, Inc. They had created a functioning local area network (LAN), and ultimately had ten IBM 3101 terminals on the system, with a lot of data stored—some of it bought on media tape from other sources, some manually input.

In 1982, with the system in place, Reed wrote to the Federal Trade Commission (FTC) requesting permission to use the information contained on the header of a credit report. The FTC returned a two-page letter, approving Reed's request, the first FTC credit-header opinion. With letter in hand, Reed contacted the credit bureaus, and with their cooperation, the credit-header product was created and is now one of the mainstays of the investigative business. By 1985, CDB Infotek and Information America began business, and the word was out. The credit-header and public records industries were moving at full steam ahead. Reed had reached his goal of providing a one-stop shopping center for public records and information sales.

Many have asked if this industry can continue to flourish and where it is headed. The best thinking today is that, with amendments to the Fair Credit Reporting Act (FCRA) due to take effect in 1997, and with self-imposed, voluntary industry standards, the original intent of the 1982 credit-header opinion letter from the FTC can still be met. Some things will change. For example, the address update based on the credit header will only return to the requester the first seven digits of a person's social security number, and with some companies none at all. But, basically, the industry will not change much, only modify itself. And the needs of the investigative and business communities will continue to be met.

OVERVIEW PATH TO ON-LINE INFORMATION BROKERS

This section is the "meat" of the book. It contains information that professional PIs (private investigators) and researchers generally will not discuss. The methods described below offer you the means of finding up to 90 percent of the American populace! On-line services are massive commercial data banks held by private companies that are in the business of selling this information. These data banks are enormous, with records totaling over 1 trillion documents! These data banks have information collated from city, county, and state records, as well as the federal government; from credit reporting bureaus; from commercial publishing firms; from commercial business reporting agencies; and from private corporate information sources. The preponderance of governmental information sold to information brokers is made up of county and state files, such as county assessor records, secretary of state filings, drivers' records, vehicle registration records, registered voters' profiles, uniform commercial codes, business licensing, fictitious business filings, liens and judgments, real property ownership, civil court filings, and criminal court filings. And it is a combination of all these sources that can lead to a successful search of a missing person.

There is no easy way to begin. This is a complex process, and I will try to simplify these on-line search techniques by providing, in a logical sequence, the most pertinent information on how to use on-line private information broker data banks.

Information brokers are professional commercial businesses that accumulate a vast array of information from numerous sources into a single set of search perimeters, easily used by you the client. Some of these data banks are news groups that tap into well over 300 newspapers, providing accurate, published information—nationwide and internationally—on people, businesses, and governments. Other data banks deal exclusively with public records, and this is the set of data banks we will discuss for finding missing persons.

There is a cost associated with the services of such information brokers, and this is how professional PIs find missing persons. All professionals spend money to find missing persons. However, you can do a simple $7 search yourself—and all you need is your computer or a fax.

Here is how the system works. Throughout the nation, there are firms that specialize in municipal, county, state, and federal public record retrieval. These public records services compile information in various formats; some formats are hard copy, and some are in media form. The larger information brokers then will buy this media when it is in electronic media form. When information is not found in electronic media form, then a smaller, specialized firm will conduct the research manually.

For example, a state may wholesale its electronic-based drivers' records to businesses. Information brokers then buy these electronic files of state drivers' records. So, when you request a search of drivers' records in a state that wholesales such records in electronic media form, it triggers an instant search of a large information broker's compiled data banks, whether you personally conduct the search or it is done by the information broker. For drivers' records searches in a state that does not wholesale its records, information brokers will subcontract this work out to small local or regional firms that specialize in state drivers' records retrieval. This search is launched with a request going from you to a large information broker. The information broker, in turn, will put this request onto a media file that is sent to this smaller firm. The specialized firm then will take this request and search the state's drivers' records data bank, under an agreement between this small firm and the state drivers' licensing unit.

Some information brokers are original buyers of information, while others "piggyback" from these original information broker buyers, and still others use a combination of the two. The first type of information broker is the original information buyer of information and generally has the most up-to-date information for resale. These original information buyers are most often the biggest companies in the industry, for example, IRSC, Inc., CDB Infotech, Inc., Information America, Inc., and Lexus-Nexus, Inc. These companies buy information from numerous sources—as many as 2,000 or more data banks in total. The data banks they acquire include government, insurance, credit, publishing, medical, and other businesses. These services have strict membership agreements and will make certain that you, the client, have legitimate access to their systems.

The second type of information brokers are those who buy from the major original information buyers and resell this information for a second time or piggyback. Now, these companies do not generally have strict client agreements. As a matter of fact, many are found on the Internet and will sell to almost anyone without a reason provided. Such firms often operate without a private investigator's license—nor are they associated with a major information trade organization, such as the Information Industry Association or the American Independent Information Professionals Association—the two big associations within the industry.

The third type of information broker is generally a private investigator who provides original *and* piggyback information for sale. These firms generally are regional in focus, hence they piggyback some information from the big original buyers of information.

Why would a state sell its records? Well, states do understand that businesses need this information in the normal conduct of business. Some of these 2,000 data banks are owned by insurance companies, others are document-retrieval services with various agreements with state governments, and others are court record services. So this myriad of data banks is as loose and varied as is the Internet itself. The private data bank services or information brokers use many of the available public data banks, and some services use all 2,000 of them!

If you're looking for access to records of more than 200 million individuals listed by previous addresses over the last seven years and by social security numbers directly on-line, here's the way to go about finding them. Terminal or Hyper-Terminal is the main source of proprietary information data banks today. It is found in the communications software of Windows 95 under the directory of accessories. Simply put, the Terminal is not the Internet or the World Wide Web. It makes your graphics-capable computer into a machine that only provides images in text format. However, the reason for Terminal usage is simple. This is the form in which proprietary information is currently available. Now, a few data banks may be found in the common Internet format of hypertext markup language or html. With Terminal you can connect to other computers and data banks and transfer files. Here's the catch: *you may connect to these proprietary data banks only as a business*, by first calling these services and setting up appropriate accounts.

All these services mandate that you must have a business. Professional information brokers expect that when they deal with you that they are dealing with another professional and that you are in business. Information brokers will only deal with businesses. This business need not be in a downtown, high-rise commercial office building, but a business nevertheless. However, a business can be run from your home. Home businesses do count! City, county, and state laws do apply, so register this business with a local government. Local governments do have fictitious business licenses for individuals to establish businesses. Many professional PIs and researchers simply operate a few telephones, a computer, and a fax machine out of their houses or apartments. Local governments provide information on starting a small home-based business, if necessary. Contact your local authorities for information.

Some of the following individual data banks have been created since 1982 and focus on countywide, state, and national searches of filings. Remember each jurisdiction is different, and not all records are available in all locations. The reasons are, first, some state and local laws and regulations may hinder information brokers from obtaining some information, and, second, the collection and reproduction methods of some small or regional retrieval companies are not always fully comprehensive. Below is a list of common data banks by jurisdiction. You will notice that city, county, and state-focused data banks are mostly governmental public records. With the nationwide-focused data banks you begin to notice a shift from governmental data banks to consumer, publishers, credit bureau, telephone, and business-related sharing of information. Only a few nationally-focused data banks are governmental, such as the National Technology Information Administration (NTIA), largely because the federal government is subject to certain privacy laws, while the states and municipalities are not. For this reason, city, county, and state public records are available in electronic media form. Of course, access to them takes longer and requires more people to retrieve and assemble this information into data banks. National data banks do not have state geographic limits, and the information found generally is business related.

Here are the locations and telephone numbers of the three largest credit bureaus within the United States. I have included telephone numbers so you can request a copy of your own credit report if you choose. Generally, if you have been denied credit, the report is free. However, sometimes the reports are free depending on state laws and the Fair Credit Reporting Act requirements. Be sure to inquire. Incidentally, when you receive your credit report, look for who has requested your report. This information will be noted at the bottom of the credit report. This report is held under federal law, so only businesses that have accounts with the bureaus or sub-bureaus can access this report, and then only with your permission. When filling out a credit application, you will see a portion of the contract that is a release for the company to check your credit report.

- Equifax, P.O. Box 740241, Atlanta, GA 30374-0241, (800) 685-1111.
  Free if credit has been denied; otherwise $8 per report in most states.
- Experian (formerly TRW), P.O. Box 2104, Allen, TX 75013-9504, (800) 682-7654.
  $8 per report in most states.
- Trans Union Corp., Consumer Relations Center, P.O. Box 390, Springfield, PA 19064-0390, (800) 888-4213. Free if credit has been denied; otherwise $8 per report in most states.

City- and County-Focused Data Banks

- FICTITIOUS BUSINESS/ASSUMED NAME DIRECTORY. Renders business name, owner name, and address of business, in addition to the filing date and file number.
- MARRIAGE INDEX—COUNTY RECORDER. Provides bride and groom name, file date, and file number based on county recorder information.
- MUNICIPAL COURT CIVIL/SMALL CLAIMS INDEX. Renders plaintiff and defendant name(s), file date, and file number.
- MUNICIPAL COURT CIVIL DIRECTORY. Provides plaintiff and defendant name(s), file date, and file number.
- MUNICIPAL COURT CRIMINAL DIRECTORY. Matches a name against a history of criminal filings to provide file date, case number, court location, and additional related information.
- REAL PROPERTY OWNERSHIP AND TRANSFER SEARCHES. Searches by property address, parcel number, or owner name to provide property description, parcel number, assessed value, transfer date, transfer amount, and property use description.
- REAL PROPERTY REFINANCE, CONSTRUCTION LOAN AND SELLER CARRY BACK RESEARCH. Searches by buyer, seller, or lender name to provide buyer name and address, seller name, lender name, loan date, loan amount, and transaction type.
- RECORDERS' DIRECTORY. Renders grantor/grantee information from county recorder files. This may include property transfers, fictitious name filings, liens and financing statements.
- REGISTERED VOTER. Matches an individual name against voter registration files to provide date of filing, file number, party affiliation, and address.
- SUPERIOR COURT CIVIL. Provides plaintiff and defendant names, file date, and case number for civil lawsuits. Most jurisdictions also include nature of the case.
- SUPERIOR COURT CRIMINAL. Searches by name to provide file date, case number, and possible alias names and charges filed.
- SUPERIOR COURT DIVORCE INDEX. Searches divorce filings to provide name of petitioner and respondent, file date, file number, and court location.
- SUPERIOR COURT PROBATE. Provides file date, file number, case title, and type of probate filed.

State-Focused Data Banks

- BANKRUPTCIES, LIENS, AND JUDGMENTS. Lists bankruptcies, federal, state, and county tax liens, and judgments filed against an individual or a business.
- CONTRACTOR LICENSE INDEX. Matches contractor license number, date of issuance, surety bond information, current status, and contractor specialization.
- CORPORATION/LIMITED PARTNERSHIP SEARCHES. Verifies corporation/ limited partnership status, inception date, and name and address of registered agent. Most states also provide officer names and business address.
- DEATH RECORD DIRECTORY. Confirms filing of a death certificate by providing file date, file number, and social security number of decedent.
- DEPARTMENT OF MOTOR VEHICLES—ALPHA NAME DIRECTORY. Provides a list of vehicles owned by an individual or business, including year, make, model, and type of vehicle. Most states also include vessels (boats).
- DEPARTMENT OF MOTOR VEHICLES—DRIVER RECORDS. Provides a history of an individual's driving performance and a description of departmental actions taken as a result of tickets or accidents. A driver's license number match and physical description are also provided.
- DEPARTMENT OF MOTOR VEHICLES—VEHICLE RECORDS. Matches registered and legal owners of a vehicle by license plate number or vehicle identification number (VIN).
- MARRIAGE INDEX. Searches by bride or groom name to provide file date and file number of a marriage certificate. May also provide age of bride and groom at the time of filing.
- PROFESSIONAL LICENSE. Verifies that an individual or business is licensed to perform specific professional services. Provides license number, date of issuance, status, and expiration dates as recorded by state authorities.
- REAL PROPERTY OWNERSHIP AND TRANSFER SEARCHES. Searches by owner name, property address, or mailing address to provide property description, parcel number, assessed value, transfer date, transfer amount, and property use description for each parcel of property owned.
- REGISTERED VOTER PROFILES. Searches statewide voter registration files to provide the name and address of a registered voter. Most states also provide voter's date of birth, gender, registration date, and party affiliation.
- STATE TAX INFORMATION. Provides correct name, owner, and address of any business holding a sales or use tax permit.
- UCC (Uniform Commercial Code) SEARCHES. Verifies that a security interest has been perfected at the state level. Includes important filing dates, file numbers, debtor, and secured party name.

Nationally-Focused Data Banks

- ADDRESS CHANGE RECORDS. Uncovers new addresses for individuals based on a three-year history of federal address changes, coupled with publisher information and mailing records from independent sources.

- ADDRESS UPDATE. Provides an individual's most current address, social security number, and year of birth based on credit profiles. This is the credit header mentioned previously.
- ADDRESS VERIFICATION. Verifies occupant name and telephone number for a desired address while uncovering occupant estimated income and length of residence. Also provides similar information for neighbors and individuals with the same last name.
- ALPHA NAME DIRECTORY. Searches 680 million files using just a subject's name, providing addresses, identifying information, demographics, and a list of neighbors. Due to the commonality of names, you can purchase names by the first 10, 20, 50, 100, or so on. The price increases in direct relation to the number of listed names.
- BUSINESS CONFIDENCE—MARKET IDENTITY. Provides company-reported sales and growth figures along with a company profile that may identify principals, years in business, and primary and secondary SIC (Standard Industrial Classification).
- BUSINESS CONFIDENCE—PAYMENT HISTORY. Details important financial information about a company, including account types, established payment terms, payment history, and average balances, as well as bankruptcies.
- CIVIL SEARCHES (DOCKET BROWSE). Searches federal, upper, or lower courts in any state to provide a history of litigation, providing plaintiff name, defendant name, file, and file number.
- CONSUMER CREDIT EMPLOYMENT REPORT. A complete consumer credit report used for employment purposes as allowed under the Federal Fair Credit Reporting Act. This report allows the employee/applicant to receive a free copy of the credit report.
- CONSUMER CREDIT REPORT. Provides address and employment information along with a listing of credit accounts, balances, credit inquiries, and payment history. This report is subject to the Federal Fair Credit Reporting Act, meaning you must have the subject's consent.
- CRIMINAL SEARCHES (DOCKET BROWSE). Searches any federal, felony, or misdemeanor criminal court by name to provide file date, case number, level of charges, and disposition. Also provides specially priced, combined major metropolitan area felony searches and nationwide felony searches.
- DUN & BRADSTREET BUSINESS INFORMATION REPORTS. Provides a business' name, address, Dun's ID number, and SIC, as well as background data about the company and its officers. In addition, important financial information is included, such as: banking references, payment histories, current assets, sales, liabilities and profits, and public filings (i.e., lawsuits, judgments, liens, and bankruptcies). In this search I should note that some of this information is volunteered by the company, so you might need to verify much in these reports for accuracy.
- FAA (Federal Aviation Administration) AIRCRAFT OWNERSHIP EXAMINATION. Displays a list of aircraft owned by an individual or a business.
- FAA (Federal Aviation Administration) LICENSE DIRECTORY. Verifies the status of an individual's pilot license. Provides address, certificate number, effective, and expiration dates.

- FEDERAL DISTRICT COURT BANKRUPTCY FILINGS. Searches by debtor name to provide open and close date, file number, and chapter of a bankruptcy petition. Additionally, in New York and Pennsylvania, the names and social security numbers of all debtors, as well as a list of docket entries, is provided.
- FEDERAL DISTRICT COURT CIVIL FILINGS. Provides open and close date, case title, and party.
- FEDERAL DISTRICT COURT CRIMINAL FILINGS. Searches by name to provide open and close date, file number, and case title for criminal cases.
- IRS ENROLLED AGENTS INQUIRY. Matches the name and address of individual enrolled tax agents who are qualified to practice tax law.
- IRS TAX PRACTITIONERS AND PREPARERS INQUIRY. This report includes the name, mailing address, and classification of individuals and businesses that either file electronic tax returns or are on the IRS's mailing list for newsletters, tax law updates, and other regularly scheduled mailings for professional tax practitioners.
- MOVING INDEX. Updates an individual's address based on information contained in consumer credit profiles.
- NATIONAL DEATH LOCATOR. Provides a decedent's name, date of birth, state of last residence, social security number, and year and state of issuance, according to Social Security Administration records. Additionally, the zip code of the death payment recipient is also provided.
- NATIONAL INFORMATION AND TECHNOLOGY ADMINISTRATION (NITA). A source for much Federal Government information.
- NEIGHBORHOOD SEARCH INDEX. Matches occupant name, phone number, and length of residence at a given address while providing similar information on up to thirty neighbors. In addition, a demographic profile of the neighborhood is included.
- OSHA (Office of Safety, Inspection, and Health) INSPECTIONS, ACCIDENTS, AND VIOLATIONS. Provides the name, address, county, and number of employees at the site of an OSHA inspection. This report may include: type of inspection, accidents, penalties, violations, failure to abate history, and so on.
- PUBLISHER'S CHANGE OF ADDRESS. Provides new address information on individuals based on changes of address filed with various magazine and publishing companies.
- SOCIAL SECURITY NUMBER TRACK SEARCHES. Provides names and addresses of all persons who have used a specific social security number for credit purposes. Often, a year of birth and spouse name or initial are included. Once again, this is the credit header mentioned earlier. This time the search is conducted in reverse fields.
- SURNAME SCAN. Matches names, addresses, and listed phone numbers of up to 200 individuals who share a common surname within a specified geographic region.
- TELEPHONE REVERSE DIRECTORY. Searches either a listed telephone number or address to confirm occupancy and match the telephone number with the address. Searches both business and residential listings.
- WATER CRAFT. The U.S. Coast Guard water craft file contains information on merchant and recreational vessels weighing no less than 5 net tons (approximately 27 feet or more) that are owned by U.S. citizens or corporations. The source for this information is the U.S. Coast Guard's Marine Safety Information System (MSIS).

Why so many data banks? What does this have to do with a missing person? Well, an investigation is a mosaic that is produced through developing numerous sources of information and, by examination and verification, moving through this web, to a labyrinth, through a maze. We never know where an investigation is going to take us. For example, if the subject I am searching for does not come up on normal name or address searches, and we have no social security number but know this individual is a pilot—bingo! We then have a lead that we can use. By running an FAA license or aircraft ownership search, we might very well find our man.

ACCESS AND GETTING HOOKED UP

The extensive commercial data banks are accessed in two ways. Entrance can be made to a few of them by use of the World Wide Web (WWW). Other methods of accessing them are as follows.

Fax Services

Fax a request to the service, and its personnel will conduct a search for you and fax back the results. Sometimes this is the best method if you are beginning and have little experience. The service personnel will assist you by providing advice on available products. Also, this type of service charges about the same amount as do the services described below.

Computer Terminal or Propriety Software

These data banks are connected through various data network providers such as SprintNet or Telnet, and you must have local telephone numbers to use these dial-up services. This is fairly easy. The staffs of these services also will provide advice on products and connections. If you are using the terminal, it is found on Windows 95 by clicking on your "Start" icon, then moving the mouse up to "Programs," then moving the mouse to "Accessories," then moving the mouse down to and clicking on "HyperTerminal." Each service has a different setting. However, the service will provide the needed settings in the agreement package they send to you. The HyperTerminal makes your powerful computer into a text-narrating word processor that cannot illustrate pictures (gif or ipg files), surf the WWW with a Netscape browser, or download file transfer protocol (ftp) and gopher files. FTP and gopher protocols transfer complete files only downloaded to be opened off line. This is not a complex communications system, but it does access commercial data banks and provides a powerful search engine for millions of records. The local telephone numbers for the connection points are provided by the information broker.

Common communications terminal software settings are unique to each service. I have included some typical settings that your terminal or HyperTerminal must be set at to connect to an on-line information broker. I have included some typical settings and tips for the use of terminal sessions.

Typical settings are changed by clicking "Start" on Windows 95; then moving the mouse to "Settings"; then clicking on "Control Panel"; then opening the modem icon; then found by clicking on "Properties"; then clicking on "Connections." Here are some common settings for use of the terminal. More specific settings and telephone numbers to information services will accompany the company's information packet.

---

1 start bit, 7 data bits, even parity, one stop bit; or
1 start bit, 8 data bits, no parity, one stop bit
9600, 13300, 28800, or 56600 BPS transmission speed
ABM/Answerback — off
Auto disconnect — off
Auto line feed — off
Block mode — off
Full duplex
Log session: On (you designate the file name)
TTY emulation; ASCII protocol; asynchronous transmission
XON/XOFF — on

Here are some additional tips on changing the port settings for a modem connection. In the HyperTerminal Connections folder, double-click the connection you want to change. Then on the "File" menu click on "Properties." Click the "Phone Number" icon, and then click on the "Configure" file. Click the "Connection" tab, and then make the changes you need. To change settings such as flow control and error correction, click "Advanced," and then make the changes necessary. Remember, each account must have a separate identity; the changes that you make to the port settings affect only this connection.

Instead of potentially losing information being downloaded to your computer, you should use capture software, so you can review the data bank information you have just accessed for a later time. While making a datafile transfer from a remote computer, use the software on the remote computer to send (download) the file to your computer. On the "Transfer" menu, click "Receive File," then type the file name path of the folder in which you want to store the file. In the "Use Receiving Protocol" box, click the protocol that the remote computer is using to send your file. You can also send the session text directly to a printer. To do this, on the "Transfer Menu," click "Capture to Printer." When you end the call, the text will be sent to your default printer.

To subscribe to a private information service, most information brokers will require a service agreement. These agreements can be intimidating, so I have enclosed a prototype copy of an information broker's service agreement so that you can familiarize yourself with its content. This type of agreement is used by all services, on-line or fax use, to protect themselves in the conduct of their businesses. The information broker is selling an information product and can have no control over the information's use once it is sold to you. So all services industry-wide have gone to this format with customers. *It does not mean they do not want to do business* but simply are holding themselves "harmless" in case a customer misuses their information product.

A typical private information broker service agreement looks like this:

Service Agreement entered into this 4th month of 25th day, 1998 by Information Broker, Information Broker and Subscriber, agrees:

1. Information Broker shall furnish to Subscriber, on request, consumer and business credit information or other data stored or accessed by computerized reporting system. Subscriber will provide Information Broker with appropriate identifying information as to itself, owners and officers of the business entity and other requested information.

2. Information Broker will exert its best efforts to deliver all information requested by Subscriber in a punctual and efficient manner. Information Broker shall have no obligation or liability to Subscriber for any delay or failure to deliver information caused or created by any third party that provides services, data or information that is delayed.

3. Subscriber hereby certifies and agrees that it will request and use any information received from Information Broker hereunder solely in connection with transactions involving the business entity for whom information is sought and will not request and use such information for non-permissible purposes prohibited by law. All such information shall be maintained by Subscriber as prescribed by law and disclosed only to employees whose duties reasonably relate to the legitimate business purposes for which the information is requested and will not sell or otherwise distribute to third parties, unless subscriber is the agent of third party, except as otherwise required by law. Further, Subscriber shall comply with all federal, state and local statutes, regulations and rules, applicable to any consumer credit information obtained or purchased by Subscriber under this Agreement, including but without limitation to the Fair Credit Reporting Act, 15 U.S.C. §1 681 et seq. ("FCRA"). Subscriber shall use credit information obtained or sold to Subscriber under this Agreement solely for Subscriber's use in connection with credit, employment or insurance underwriting transactions between a third party and a consumer to whom the credit information relates and for other permissible purposes as defined under FCRA.

4. The Information Broker shall exercise reasonable efforts to furnish to the Subscriber accurate information. Both Information Broker and Subscriber hereby agree that the limitation of Information Broker's total liability to Subscriber under this Agreement shall be the return of the fees paid by Subscriber for the data accessed to the extent said data and information is found to be the primary basis upon which the Subscriber incurred any injury or damage resulting from the furnishing of such information but shall not be liable to Subscriber for any other damages whatsoever, including punitive damages, exemplary damages, consequential damages, or any other costs and expenses whatsoever except as expressly agreed to herein above. Limitation of liability provided for herein above shall not apply in the event of any negligence or intentional wrongdoing in transmitting data pursuant to the terms of this Agreement. Subscriber acknowledges that all data and information provided and/or sold to Subscriber under this Agreement is purchased "as is."

5. Subscriber shall indemnify, defend, and hold harmless Information Broker from and against any and all costs, expenses and liabilities which may be paid by or assessed against Information Broker based upon the illegal use by Subscriber of credit or any other information furnished to Subscriber by Information Broker.

6. For each response to a request for information (including "no hit"), Subscriber agrees to pay Information Broker the pre-disclosed charge for the various services rendered to Subscriber via a pre-charged Mastercard/Visa account. Such charges will be specified in Information Broker's published Service List and/or on-line system and are subject to change with notice.

7. This Agreement is deemed made in the State of California, and shall be construed in accordance with the laws of the State of California.

8. Information Broker represents and warrants that its activities in collection and reporting of credit and other information are conducted consistent with all applicable law and regulation.

9. Information Broker does not guarantee or warrant the correctness or completeness of any information products and shall not be liable to Subscriber for any loss, damage, lost profits, injury, or death caused in whole or part due to any product the Information Broker provides.

FORM 4.1 Subscriber Service Agreement

PRODUCTS AND PRICING

Pricing in this industry has come way down within the past few years as a result of the glut of new firms selling information in this field. In years past, an address update or social security number trace, commonly known as credit headers, would cost $15 to $20 each. Now they cost only around $7 to $9 each. Pricing per search varies from service to service and by complexity of search. Cost variance is due to the effort and expense the information broker must incur to collate these files into a single data bank. In the case of Department of Motor Vehicle (DMV) records, magnetic files from the states can range in price from $120 to thousands of dollars, so the rate per record varies. Some states sell updates every quarter or every month, so this increases the price as well. In the case of DMV, and for that matter all records, the prices vary greatly due to revisions from the issuing agency.

For the pricing pages below, understand that address update source reports and social security traces are the credit headers described in Chapter 1. Credit header traces represent one of the best tools an investigator has and produces the name, address, social security number, and sometimes the telephone number of an individual.

TYPICAL SEARCH REQUEST REQUIREMENTS AND OUTCOME REPORTS

Information brokers have numerous products, and here I will describe them in detail and provide examples of the results—the search outcome report. One of my first search outcome reports from an information broker uncovered the new address of an individual. This new address led to a civil law case being filed in a sexual harassment suit. That gave me a good deal of satisfaction as a member of the investigative community and, in turn, led to making someone account for their suspected illegal actions.

Based upon your request for a report, the outcome will vary in content. It is impossible to list all the outcome reports here, but I have cited a few that might give you an idea of the outcome. Not all services are equal, so different information brokers might provide you with different results, and variations sometimes do appear. Such deviations occur generally when one service uses a data bank that has not been updated or is out-of-date. For this reason, I always recommend using a time-tested information broker who has at least five years of business experience. Let's begin with a few typical reports.

Address Update Example (Credit Header)

TYPICAL PRICE: $7, could be as low as $1.50 per report.

PRODUCT COMMENTS: Equifax or TransUnion or TRW

RETURN TIME: Immediate on-line or fax-back service available

Additional Comments: You can get all three, Equifax or TransUnion or TRW, for somewhere around $17 to $23.

Address Update. This product is the famous credit header, which can provide a subject and spouse's initial, current, and previous addresses, social security numbers, and other information that is found in credit files. This search is invaluable as a location tool if you only have a name and a previous address, since it can provide you with a subject's social security number. However, federal regulations may soon result in modifying this provision to providing only the first seven digits of the social security number.

Search techniques: A previous address may often be used to locate a subject's current address. It is very simple. You can simply query a number of very large nationwide data banks immediately, returning every occurrence of that name and address, as well as the names and addresses and social security numbers associated with it. Included is a date that the information was reported, helping not only to verify previous addresses, but to establish the subject's current length of residence.

Characteristics that will increase search success: The person you are looking for should be at least eighteen or nineteen years of age or older. A person needs to have time to "get into the system." Having good or bad credit is one way to get into it. Be sure the person has been "away" from the previous address for at least two months before trying this search—in order for the subject to establish a record of a new address. Double-check your information. In a case requiring this kind of investment, there is no room for error. This is a great product!

With the credit header, we requested updated address information on Mary S. Houghton, 345 S. Diablo, Oakland, CA 95301. All we had was a former address, and this name and address was the basis for a credit header using a name and address search. The outcome report delivered to us provided Mary S. Houghton's new address of 5147 -3ᴿᴰ

Requisite Data Entry: Name, Previous Address

Date: May 07 03-.08:48 AM 1994 Inquiry Number 98
1 05/07/97   12:05:22   CB01   906 BAV4

INPUT DATA: Mary S. Houghton
          345 S. Diablo, Oakland, CA 95301

****FILE IDENT-.SS# IS 123-45-67xx   YOB IS 1961   SPOUSE FREDERICK L. (415) 123-4567

1-97   Mary S. Houghton
1   5147 -3ᴿᴰ STREET, APT 4, SAN FRANCISCO, CA 94105

        ****ATTN: FILE VARIATION: ZIP IS 94105
OTHER FILE IDENT: MID INIT IS S

2-97   Mary S. Houghton
        5147 -3ᴿᴰ STREET, APT 4, SAN FRANCISCO, CA 94105

4-93   Mary S. Houghton
        345 S. Diablo, Oakland, CA 95301

8-92   Mary S. Houghton
        1410 E. Helaman Court, Chicago, IL 60631

ADDRESS LOCATED REPORT TYPE P NOT TO BE USED FOR CREDIT GRANTING.

END OF REPORT

FORM 4.2   Address update search results might look like this.

Street, Apartment 4, San Francisco, CA 94105. In addition, we know from the report that the last time a credit company listed her at this address was in February 1997.

So, in this case, the report stipulates that as of February 1997, Mary S. Houghton received and paid her credit bill from this address. Of course, a variable might exist, and this would be that Mary's mail is being forwarded. So we must verify this information by attempting to call the address. In this case, the telephone number of (415) 123-4567 is listed, too. So by calling this number we hope to find Mary or her husband Frederick there. If so, the information is verified. If the last month of location was more than a year old, we might need to verify if the telephone is being forwarded as well. But normally in cases like this, unless the person is on the run, the information is reliable but needs to be verified. This report even uncovers approximate dates for two other locations, so if she has moved from the first address, then these other addresses provide a lead. Remember, this report has a time limitation generally of seven years.

Bankruptcies, Liens, and Judgments

TYPICAL PRICE: $13 by state or $15 by court

PRODUCT COMMENTS: By court or by state

RETURN TIME: 1–3 days

The bankruptcies, liens, and judgments search can provide information from the state requested on an individual or a business. This information can be useful to identify debtor addressees and financial liabilities. Below is a description of jurisdictions that can be searched individually. Searches are conducted by state only; national searches are not available.

Requisite Data Entry: Individual or Business Name, by State

NAME: Mary S. Houghton
SS#:   5156-3439
DOB: 11/01/61

COUNTY/STATE CHECKED:	SAN FRANCISCO, CA
DATE CHECKED:	11-22-93
CHECKED BY:	LP
YEARS CHECKED:	7
ALIAS:	NO

Lien # 12-39487, Alexandria and Hephaistion Roofing Company
Property, 4353 Green Street, San Francisco, CA

END OF REPORT

FORM 4.3   Court search results might look like this.

Courts within the United States Available for Search

Alabama
Middle Bankruptcy Court
Northern Bankruptcy Court—Anniston
Northern Bankruptcy Court—Birmingham
Northern Bankruptcy Court—Decatur
Northern Bankruptcy Court—Tuscaloosa
Northern District Court
Southern Bankruptcy Court
Southern District Court

Alaska
Bankruptcy Court

Arizona
Bankruptcy Court—Phoenix
Bankruptcy Court—Tucson
Bankruptcy Court—Yuma
District Court

Arkansas
Bankruptcy Court
Eastern District Court

California
Central-San Bernardino Bankruptcy Court
Central-Santa Ana Bankruptcy Court
Central-Santa Barbara Bankruptcy Court
Central District Court
Eastern Bankruptcy Court
Northern Bankruptcy Court
Southern Bankruptcy Court
Southern District Court

Colorado
Bankruptcy Court
District Court

Connecticut
Bankruptcy Court
District Court

Delaware
Bankruptcy Court
District Court

District of Columbia
Bankruptcy Court
District Court

Florida
Middle Bankruptcy Court—
    Jacksonville
Middle Bankruptcy Court—Orlando
Middle Bankruptcy Court—Tampa
Middle District Court
Southern Bankruptcy Court
Southern District Court

Georgia
Middle Bankruptcy Court
Northern Bankruptcy Court
Northern District Court
Southern Bankruptcy Court—Augusta
Southern Bankruptcy Court—
    Savannah
Southern District Court

Hawaii
Bankruptcy Court
District Court

Idaho
Bankruptcy Court
District Court

Illinois
Central Bankruptcy Court
Central District Court
Northern Bankruptcy Court—
    Chicago
Northern Bankruptcy Court—
    Rockford
Northern District Court
Southern Bankruptcy Court
Southern District Court

Indiana
Northern Bankruptcy Court
Northern District Court

Iowa
Northern Bankruptcy Court
Southern Bankruptcy Court
Southern District Court

Kansas
Bankruptcy Court

Kentucky
Eastern Bankruptcy Court
Eastern District Court
Western Bankruptcy Court
Western District Court

Louisiana
Eastern Bankruptcy Court
Eastern District Court
Middle District Court
Western Bankruptcy Court
Western District Court

Maine
Bankruptcy Court
District Court

Maryland
Bankruptcy Court
District Court

Massachusetts
Bankruptcy Court
District Court

Michigan
Eastern Bankruptcy Court
Eastern District Court
Western Bankruptcy Court
Western District Court

Minnesota
Bankruptcy Court
District Court

Mississippi
Northern Bankruptcy Court
Northern District Court

Southern Bankruptcy Court—Biloxi
Southern Bankruptcy Court—Jackson

Missouri
Eastern Bankruptcy Court
Eastern District Court
Western Consolidated Court

Montana
Bankruptcy Court
District Court

Nebraska
Bankruptcy Court
District Court

Nevada
Bankruptcy Court

New Hampshire
Bankruptcy Court
District Court

New Jersey
Bankruptcy Court
District Court

New Mexico
Bankruptcy Court
District Court

New York
Eastern Bankruptcy Court
Eastern District Court
Northern Bankruptcy Court
Northern District Court
Southern Bankruptcy Court
Southern District Court
Western Bankruptcy Court
Western District Court

North Carolina
Eastern District Court
Middle Bankruptcy Court
Middle District Court
Western Bankruptcy Court

North Dakota
Bankruptcy Court
District Court

Ohio
Northern Bankruptcy Court
Northern District Court
Southern Bankruptcy Court
Southern District Court

Oklahoma
Eastern Bankruptcy Court
Northern Bankruptcy Court
Northern District Court
Western Bankruptcy Court
Western District Court

Oregon
Bankruptcy Court
District Court

Pennsylvania
Middle Bankruptcy Court—Harrisburg
Middle Bankruptcy Court—Wilkes-Barre
Western Bankruptcy Court
Western District Court

Puerto Rico
Bankruptcy Court
District Court

Rhode Island
Bankruptcy Court
District Court

South Carolina
Bankruptcy Court
District Court

South Dakota
Bankruptcy Court

Tennessee
Eastern Bankruptcy Court
Middle District Court

Western Bankruptcy Court
Western District Court

Texas
Eastern Bankruptcy Court
Eastern District Court
Northern Bankruptcy Court
Northern District Court
Southern Consolidated Court
Western Bankruptcy Court
Western District Court

Utah
Bankruptcy Court
District Court

Vermont
Bankruptcy Court
District Court

Virginia
Eastern Bankruptcy Court—
  Alexandria
Eastern Bankruptcy Court—Norfolk
Eastern Bankruptcy Court—
  Richmond
Eastern Bankruptcy Court—Newport
  News
Eastern District Court

Washington
Eastern Bankruptcy Court
Eastern District Court
Western Bankruptcy Court
Western District Court

West Virginia
Northern Bankruptcy Court
Southern Bankruptcy Court

Wisconsin
Eastern Bankruptcy Court
Western Bankruptcy Court
Western District Court

Wyoming
Bankruptcy Court

Civil Court Records

TYPICAL PRICE: $19

PRODUCT COMMENTS: By court or county

RETURN TIME: 1–4 days

Civil Court Records.   This report is designed to provide case docket information on current or previous civil court cases pertaining to a company or an individual by court or county. Interestingly enough, this report result may include law firms involved in the case.

Commercial Business Profiles

TYPICAL PRICE: $45

PRODUCT COMMENTS: By state

RETURN TIME: 1–4 days

Commercial Business Profiles.   This product report is designed to describe a business's credit history, profit and loss history, length of business, type of business, officers, banking and loan references, payment trends, number of employees, sales volume, and other information. This report is much like the famous Dun and Bradstreet reports for businesses. Remember, some information is voluntarily provided by the business itself

---

Requisite Data Entry: Name, Court to Search

NAME: Mary S. Houghton
SS#:   5156-3439
DOB: 11/01/61

COUNTY/STATE CHECKED:	SAN FRANCISCO, CA
DATE CHECKED:	11-22-93
CHECKED BY:	LP
YEARS CHECKED:	7
ALIAS:	NO
CIVIL #1:	Bradford Insurance vs. Houghton, Insurance, Automobile
DISP:	Bradford # Doc.812497
CIVIL #2:	Houghton vs. Bank of Swaziborough, Funds Transfer, Property
DISP:	Houghton # Doc.19871
END OF REPORT	

FORM 4.4   Civil court records search results might look like this.

Requisite Data Entry: Business Name and Address

The Hephaistion Company, Inc.　　Number: 60-453-5354

Address:	51565 Union Street, San Francisco, CA 94117
Telephone:	415 123-1234
Sales:	$6,504,345 (Projected) (F)
Net Worth:	$1,234,445 (F)

DESCRIPTION OF DATA RANKINGS
Year Started: March 11, 1991
Control Year: 1969
This is a Headquarters location.
Employees Here: 14
Employees Total: 34
Top Executive: HOUGHTON, MARY S., PRES.

INDUSTRY
Line of Business: Commercial Printing and Consulting
Primary SIC: 2752 (Commercial printing, lithographic)
Extended SIC: 0965 (Speaking Service)

SPECIAL EVENTS
02/11/97 On Sept. 9, 1997, the company experienced a water leak. According to Mary Houghton, President, damages amounted to $87,000, which were fully covered by their insurance company. The business was closed for fourteen days due to the water damage.

12/17/96 Company moved from 9012 Green Street to 51565 Union Street on December 12, 1996.

BUSINESS HISTORY - 07/24/96
HOUGHTON, PRES; WILLIAM S. ALEXANDER, SEC-TREAS; DIRECTOR(S): THE OFFICER(S)

BUSINESS TYPE: Corporation - Profit
DATE INCORPORATED: 05/21/1991
AUTH SHARES - COMMON: 500
STATE OF INCORP: California
PAR VALUE - COMMON: No Par Value

Business started March 11, 1991 by HOUGHTON AND WILLIAM S. ALEXANDER. 100% of capital stock is owned by officers. HOUGHTON born 1961. Graduated from the University of California, Berkeley, in May 1983 with a BS degree in Engineering. 1987-91 production manager for Diload Engineering, Palm Desert, CA.

HEPHAISTION born 1957. Graduated from Western Illinois University, Macomb, IL in May 1978. 1981-1991 was Political Advisor to The Smith Institute of Fremont, CA

OPERATIONS
05/09/96 Subsidiary of Hephaistion Leasing Company, Inc., Fremont, CA, started 1991 which operates as a holding company for its subsidiaries. Parent company owns 100% of capital stock. Parent company has 5 other subsidiaries. Intercompany relations: consist of automobile leasing contracts. A consolidated financial statement of the parent company dated Dec. 31, 1996, showed a worth of $1,456,666, with an overall fair financial condition. Commercial printing specializing in marketing brochures, annual reports, book publication, and CEO speech writing. Has 175 account(s). Net 30 days. Sells to commercial concerns.

Territory: United States.
EMPLOYEES: 34 employed here, including officers.
FACILITIES: Rents 7,345 sq. ft. on second floor of fourteen-story concrete CMU building in good condition.
LOCATION: Central business section on well-traveled street.
BRANCHES: None

END OF REPORT

FORM 4.5　Commercial business profile search results might look like this.

and must be verified for authenticity. On-line Dun and Bradstreet offer this same product for member companies at $20 a report at http://www.dbisna.com/. I like these reports. However, they are not generally applicable to missing persons cases, but certainly are for business asset investigations.

Corporation Affiliated with Other Companies

TYPICAL PRICE: $45 to $65
PRODUCT COMMENTS: By state
RETURN TIME: 1–4 days

Corporation Affiliated with Other Companies.   This report can provide information on the true ownership of a company, generally when one corporation owns another. This search might identify a corporate affiliation and list various business details as well. This product is available only for some states.

Corporation Records

TYPICAL PRICE: $55
PRODUCT COMMENTS: By state
RETURN TIME: 1–4 days

Requisite Data Entry: Company Name, Address

NAME: Houghton Industries
Tax Number: 45-0813
DOB: 11/01/61

STATE CHECKED: CA
DATE CHECKED: 11-22-96
CHECKED BY: LP
YEARS CHECKED: 7

The Hephaistion Company, Corporate CA filing # 12-098, 05-04-96, Limited Project Partnership

The Hephaistion Company, Inc., Number: 60-453-5354, 51565 Union Street, San Francisco, CA 94117
Telephone: 415 123-1234

END OF REPORT

FORM 4.6   Corporation affiliated with other companies search results might look like this.

Requisite Data Entry: Company Name, Address

NAME: Houghton Industries
Tax number: 234-4981
Date of incorporation: 14/16/96

STATE CHECKED: CA
DATE CHECKED: 11-22-96
CHECKED BY: PP
YEARS CHECKED: 7

14593 Union Street, San Francisco, CA 94154, (415) 123-4567
Registered Agent: Mary S. Houghton, 494 Green Street, San Francisco, CA 94131

END OF REPORT

FORM 4.7   Corporations records search results might look like this.

Corporation Records.   The product will produce a corporate records search by state, including corporate records filed by state corporations with the Secretary of State's Office. The record is likely to produce the name of business, date incorporated, addresses, officers, type or corporation, registered agent, and sometimes provides the name of the person or attorney who filed the papers. This product is only available in some states.

A reverse search of this same report would be a search by registered agent name by state. This requires a name and state field parameter. The results would be the same and cost about the same.

Criminal Record Example

TYPICAL PRICE: See Table 4.1

PRODUCT COMMENTS: By county or state, as applicable

RETURN TIME: 1 day

Criminal Records Search.   This search can be done by county or statewide. Note below that this is not available for all states. The reason is that state laws prohibit release of criminal records from some states. This search can be used to learn if someone is or has been convicted of a crime—great if you want to check out your new baby-sitter.

I'd guess that anyone reading this report would conclude that Mary has been naughty! This search is conducted by name and county. Sorry, folks, but if you think we can use national law enforcement computers, not so. This search is done by the use of criminal filings by county. At the courthouse you can view these records just by asking for them. But they are also compiled by county, and the search field is the name. At the county level these records might occasionally be listed in one case with the middle initial and in another case without the middle initial. So you can see that, at times, not all relevant data

TABLE 4.1 Typical price for a criminal record search.

STATE	COUNTY	STATEWIDE
ALASKA (AK)	11.00	N/A
ALABAMA (AL)	11.00	60.00
ARKANSAS (AR)	11.00	40.00
ARIZONA (AZ)	11.00	N/A
CALIFORNIA (CA)	11.00	N/A
COLORADO (CO)	11.00	19.00
CONNECTICUT (CT)	N/A	N/A
DISTRICT OF COLUMBIA (DC)	N/A	15.00
DELAWARE (DE)	11.00	N/A
FLORIDA (FL)	14.00	35.00 1–3 Days
GEORGIA (GA)	11.00	33.00 1 Day
HAWAII (HI)	11.00	N/A
IOWA (IA)	11.00	N/A
IDAHO (ID)	11.00	30.00
ILLINOIS (IL)	11.00	37.00
INDIANA (IN)	11.00	33.00
KANSAS (KS)	11.00	37.00
KENTUCKY (KY)	11.00	N/A
LOUISIANA (LA)	11.00	N/A
MASSACHUSETTS (MA)	11.00	N/A
MARYLAND (MD)	11.00	N/A
MAINE (ME)	11.00	33.00
MICHIGAN (MI)	11.00	30.00
MINNESOTA (MN)	11.00	34.00
MISSOURI (MO)	11.00	30.00
MISSISSIPPI (MS)	11.00	N/A
MONTANA (MT)	11.00	30.00
NORTH CAROLINA (NC)	11.00	N/A
NORTH DAKOTA (ND)	11.00	51.00
NEBRASKA (NE)	11.00	37.00
NEW HAMPSHIRE (NH)	11.00	N/A
NEW JERSEY (NJ)	11.00	N/A
NEW MEXICO (NM)	11.00	30.00
NEVADA (NV)	11.00	N/A
NEW YORK (NY)	11.00	N/A

Continued

TABLE 4.1   Continued

STATE	COUNTY	STATEWIDE
OHIO (OH)	11.00	N/A
OKLAHOMA (OK)	11.00	37.00
OREGON (OR)	11.00	40.00
PENNSYLVANIA (PA)	11.00	37.00
RHODE ISLAND (RI)	11.00	N/A
SOUTH CAROLINA (SC)	11.00	45.00
SOUTH DAKOTA (SD)	11.00	N/A
TENNESSEE (TN)	11.00	N/A
TEXAS (TX)	11.00	N/A
UTAH (UT)	11.00	N/A
VIRGINIA (VA)	11.00	37.00
VERMONT (VT)	11.00	N/A
WASHINGTON (WA)	11.00	37.00
WISCONSIN (WI)	11.00	37.00
WEST VIRGINIA (WV)	11.00	N/A
WYOMING (WY)	11.00	N/A

Requisite Data Entry: Name and Date of Birth

NAME: Mary S. Houghton
SS#:   5156-3439
DOB: 11/01/61

COUNTY/STATE CHECKED: SAN FRANCISCO, CA

DATE CHECKED: 11-22-93
CHECKED BY: LP
YEARS CHECKED: 7
ALIAS: NO

CHARGE #1:   DRIVING UNDER THE INFLUENCE
DISP: CONVICTED - 6 MOS. PROBATION

CHARGE #2:   FRAUD-INSUFFICIENT FUNDS CHECK
DISP: CONVICTED - 6 MOS. PROBATION

CHARGE #3:   STOLEN VEHICLE-FAILURE TO RE-DELIVER HIRED VEHICLE
DISP: CONVICTED - $800.00

CHARGE #4:   FRAUD BY DECEPTION
DISP: CONVICTED - $5,500 FINE

END OF REPORT

FORM 4.8   Criminal record search results might look like this.

will show up. I also like manual searching, since I can view various last names, first names, and middle name/initial combinations on the county courthouse's computer.

Death Record Search

TYPICAL PRICE: $6
PRODUCT COMMENTS: National
RETURN TIME: Immediate on-line or fax-back service available.

Death Record Search.   This product can produce the date of death and some added information. The information needed for this search could be numerous forms of field parameters, such as first name, last name, and date of birth or death, or social security number. Some data banks have over 47 million of these records, and the database is updated every three months. Remember that there are similar free products on the Internet! I can attest to the accuracy of the free Internet products.

Driving Record Example

TYPICAL PRICE: $9 to $19 (A.N.I. search approximately $35, return time 1–30 days)
PRODUCT COMMENTS: By state
RETURN TIME: 1–4 days

Numerous products can provide information on driving records or registrations. Generally they access the same data bank, but with different search field parameters, producing the same information.

Requisite Data Entry: SSN or Date of Death or Date of Birth and Name
INPUT
Houghton, Mary S.
Social Security Number: 123-45-5678

DATA SEARCH
Date of death   02/03/1994
Los Angeles, CA
Death certificate number   3245-352345

END OF REPORT

FORM 4.9   Death record search results might look like this.

Alpha Search (A.N.I.).   This product is good if the subject's license plate or VIN number is unknown. By providing a subject's name, date of birth, or social security number, this report can produce all the vehicles registered to a subject in a particular state.

Requisite Data Entry: Name, SSN, or Date of Birth and the State to Search

Driving Record—Name, DOB, State.   This search is designed to yield an individual's driving record for an individual state, but it's not available in all states. Sometimes inquiries produce an "inquiry notice" of an individual's driving record, depending on state laws. This product is not available in all states.

Requisite Data Entry: Name, Date of Birth, and State to Search

License Plate Registrations.   Nationwide license plate identification search, provided from any plate/tag number you request and the state to be searched, to determine

---

Requisite Data Entry: License Plate Number, State

MVR REQUEST FROM: SAN FRANCISCO, CA   REPORT DATE: 03/24/97

NAME: Mary S. Houghton   MVR REQUESTED AS: DL#: 123-76-678
5147 -3RD STREET, APT 4, SAN FRANCISCO, CA 94105

DRIVERS LICENSE NO. 123-76-678   DATE OF BIRTH 02/01/67   ISSUED DATE 01/03/87
          EXPIRE DATE   01/02/99   SSN: 123-45-6789
SEX: F
HEIGHT: 5'7"
WEIGHT: 145
EYES: Blue
HAIR: Blonde
ALIAS NAME: None
PREVIOUS LICENSE NO.:   NC 24562
LICENSE TYPE/CLASS: C
STATUS: Valid
RESTRICTIONS: Glasses
VIOLATION: Driving too fast for conditions
VIOLATION/SUSPENTION: VC565
TYPE: Moving
DATE: 11/01/95
VIOLATION DESCRIPTION: Paid
ACCD   ACCIDENT(PERS INJ) ON 03-2-91

END MVR RECORD

FORM 4.10   Driving record search results might look like this.

the ownership of the vehicle and all addresses assigned to that plate number and its VIN number.

Once again, Mary has been misbehaving! This report is based on search fields of name and address and has produced a complete state driver's record. Since all the records are listed by driver license number, the report is valid but not necessarily complete. This report will not include other states' driving violations on another license number. This report provides us with physical characteristics of Mary, along with behavior reporting. Notice that Mary wears glasses! Remember, people move sometimes and do not report to the Department of Motor Vehicles their new locations, so this report is better suited for drivers' information and physical characteristics only. For an updated address, the credit header is still the best report.

Education Verification Example

TYPICAL PRICE: $13
PRODUCT COMMENTS: None
RETURN TIME: 1–4 days

Education Verification.   This search is intended to confirm colleges attended, dates, degree, and other information as available.

This report can be done by yourself by pretexting. Educational verification is achieved quite simply by the use of your telephone, then written into report form as seen below. Some data banks do exist for this purpose.

Requisite Data Entry: Name, Address, SSN, Date of Birth, College and Years Attended

EDUCATION VERIFICATION
NAME: Mary S. Houghton

DATE OF BIRTH:	1950
SOCIAL SECURITY:	123-45-6789
NAME OF SCHOOL ATTENDED:	UNIVERSITY OF CALIFORNIA, BERKELEY
DEGREES OBTAINED:	BSE-IND
YEARS ATTENDED:	1978 TO 1982
STUDIES:	ENGINEERING

END OF REPORT

FORM 4.11   Education verification search results might look like this.

Fictitious Business Names Search

TYPICAL PRICE: $15

PRODUCT COMMENTS: By individual name or business name for a countywide search

RETURN TIME: 1–2 days

Fictitious Business Names Search.   The fictitious business name search is intended to search for and to provide information that reflects the filings of an individual or company to conduct business under a fictitious business name within a given county. Information returned can include owner's name, business name, file date, and file number and in most areas business address. Availability currently includes nationwide files searched by state.

Requisite Data Entry: Individual or Business Name, County to Search

Marriage License Search

TYPICAL PRICE: $9+

PRODUCT COMMENTS: By county or state

RETURN TIME: 1–4 days

Marriage License Search.   The marriage license search is intended to provide a search of marriage records in the requested county or state. Remember that all this information is input by people, so verification is necessary. Information that might be returned can include filing date, registration number (or book and page number), spouse's name, and in some areas the age of the bride and/or groom. Availability currently includes California, Arizona, and Nevada.

Requisite Data Entry: Individual Name, County or State to Search

National Change-of-Address Search

TYPICAL PRICE: $10

PRODUCT COMMENTS: Options include with five neighbors or ten neighbors

RETURN TIME: Immediate on-line search or by fax-back

National Change-of-Address Search.   Although this report could be based on many data sources, for this example we will suppose it is based on publisher's information. The report might return forwarding address information and telephone number information on

---

Requisite Data Entry: Full Name, Previous Address

Date: May 07 03-.08:48 AM 1994   Inquiry Number   98
1 05/07/97 12:05:22
INPUT DATA: Mary S. Houghton
                                     345 S. Diablo, Oakland, CA 95301

Updated: Mary S. Houghton
                                     5147 -3RD STREET, APT 4, SAN FRANCISCO, CA 94105

END OF REPORT

FORM 4.12   National change-of-address search results might look like this.

a subject. You can also select the option to return the addresses and telephone numbers of five or ten of the subject's neighbors. It is my opinion that the credit header is often superior to publisher's information. However, I am always tracked by Publisher's Clearing House for my chance to win $10 million. The combination of publisher's and credit header data banks makes for outstanding results, but you should always ask what the source is.

Professional License Verification

TYPICAL PRICE: $17

PRODUCT COMMENTS: By state, generally 30–50 licenses searched

RETURN TIME: Some firms are on-line with this information, others fax back in 1–3
  days.

Professional License Verification.   Generally this search, depending on the information broker, can be conducted by category or by state (all categories). For example, each board listed might have many variations and as many as fifty licenses: accountants, architectural examiners, behavioral science examiners, collections and investigative services, barbers and cosmetologists, dental examiners, dental auxiliaries, dentists, electronic and appliance repair services, funeral directors and embalmers, geologists and geophysicists, furnishings and thermal insulation, dry cleaners, architects, medical board, dispensing opticians, acupuncturist, nursing home administrators, hearing aid dispenser examiners, physical therapists, optometrists, physician assistants, podiatrists, pharmacists, psychologists, professional engineers and land surveyors, respiratory care examiners, speech pathologists and audio examiners, registered nurses, shorthand reporters, structural pest services, chiropractic examiners, tax-preparers, veterinarians, animal health technician examiners, and psychiatric technician examiners.

Requisite Data Entry: Name, Address, DOB, State to Be Searched

Date: May 07 03-.08:48 AM 1994   Inquiry Number   98
1 05/07/97   12:05:22

INPUT DATA: Mary S. Houghton, California, DOB 11/01/61

License: Practical Nurse, expires 11/01/99, first issued 11/01/90

Updated: Mary S. Houghton
                               5147 -3ᴿᴰ STREET, APT 4, SAN FRANCISCO, CA 94105

END OF REPORT

FORM 4.13   Professional license verification search results might look like this.

Real Property Asset Search Example

TYPICAL PRICE: $12 to $30

PRODUCT COMMENTS: By state or county

RETURN TIME: Some firms are on-line with this information, others fax back in 1–3 days.

Real Property Asset Search.   This search product is designed to determine ownership of property, where property is located, type of property, book, parcel numbers, assessed value, and other information.

I really like this type of report for asset investigations. This report tells you a lot about the property and sales price, including the sales history of the property. Of course, you can acquire the information at the assessor's office at the county government level, but this report will provide the same information. This is really an extensive report.

Registered Voter Searches

TYPICAL PRICE: $16

PRODUCT COMMENTS: No-hit fee is sometimes around $7; this search is by county or by state.

RETURN TIME: Some firms are on-line with this information, others fax back in 1–3 days.

Registered Voter Searches.   This search product examines a state's voter registration records. This product can be used to obtain an address and/or county of residence for an individual. This report in some states has restrictions, but where available, this report is extensive and can include information such as: individual's name and residence address,

Requisite Data Entry: Name or Street Address or Parcel Number

APN :199-92-960   Use: SFR   County: SAN FRANCISCO, CA

Property: 1996 N HIGH STREET, SAN FRANCISCO, CA 94131 RRO7

Owner Mary S. Houghton   Phone : 602-345-6798
Mail   5147 -3RD STREET, APT 4, SAN FRANCISCO, CA 94105

PROPERTY DATA   CURRENT SALES DATA   ASSESSMENT DATA:

BldgSF   2343
SalePr $264,000
Total FCV: $256,448
Yrbit :   1986
$/SqFt $169
Land FCV: $125,000
Stories: 1
RecDate: 09/20/93
Impr FCV: $331,448
Rooms   7
Doc#:   92-928919
%improved: 84%
Bath/FX: 4/12
DocType: JOINT TENANCY
TaxAmount: $2,058.23
Garage   GARAGE2
CashDwn: $16,600
Tax Year: 96
Pool :   N
Mtg Amt: $147,400A
Tax Area :   9941
Heating: FORCED AIR
Finance: HIGHBNK
Census: 2358.05
A/C; REFRIGERATION;
Roof: ASHP

PRIOR SALES DATA: 1987 Doc# SF097815
TRANSFER DATA: 1988 Doc# 0954245
ExtWall: FRAME WOOD
SalePr $359,900
Seller: SMITH R.
TypeImp: RS3
$/SqFt $168
Doc#:   758390
LCIC: 01-31
RecDate: 04/30/87
DocTyp: JNT TEN
Doc   87-267838
Land SF : 4567   DocType: JOINT TENANCY
ParcelSZ: 1   Mtg Amt: $137,000
Finance: INTRMG
Legal Lot: 14
Legal Block: 1
Legal Tract: TRS:4889
Legal   SAN FRANCISCO, CA FINAL PLAT NO 572
Comments: PRIMASMT: $35,140; SECASMT: $35,140; ASSESS: 10%; TOTLTD: $156,448; LCIC:
SINGLE FAM UNIT; TYPEIMP: SFR; CLASS: R3; GRADE: GOOD; CONDITION: AVE;

FORM 4.14   Real property asset search results might look like this.

Requisite Data Entry: Full Name and Address

Date: May 07 05:08:52 AM 1997   Inquiry Number   89

PAGE 1

DATE 5-07-94   TIME 17:08:54   PPE15 V580

Mary S. Houghton   11/01/1966

5147 -3RD STREET, APT 4, SAN FRANCISCO, CA 94105
(415) 123-4567
Sex: Female
Race: Other
Party: Independent
Occupation: Registered Nurse
Other household: Michael P. Johnson

END OF REPORT

FORM 4.15   Registered voter search results might look like this.

phone number, voter registration number, county and party affiliation, and additional household member(s). Many states also include the individual's date of birth, gender, race, head of household name, and other household members. Some states are not available or have restrictions.

Social Security Number Search Example

TYPICAL PRICE: $7, could be as low as $1.50 per report.

PRODUCT COMMENTS: National credit header search

RETURN TIME: On-line

Social Security Search.   This search is the address update (credit header) in reverse. This report is input by field parameters of social security number only. It will let you know if the number has been linked with potentially fraudulent activity, or if this social security number has been reported as that of a deceased person.

This report is the same as the address update report. The difference is that the search field was the social security number, not a name and address. This report will deliver all those people that are using the social security number for credit purposes. This is important for another reason than just an address update. It will tell you if someone else is using your social security number. If different names come up on this report, then we know that different names have been used to obtain credit. Suspicious? I'd be! As the address update, this report provides all known residences for a time period of approximately seven years. Table 4.2 explains the meaning of the first three digits of a social security number.

TABLE 4.2 First Digits of Social Security Number Identification by State.

FIRST THREE DIGITS	*STATE*
001–003	NEW HAMPSHIRE
004–007	MAINE
008–009	VERMONT
010–034	MASSACHUSETTS
035–039	RHODE ISLAND
040–049	CONNECTICUT
050–134	NEW YORK
135–158	NEW JERSEY
159–211	PENNSYLVANIA
212–220	MARYLAND
221–222	DELAWARE
223–231	VIRGINIA
232–236	WEST VIRGINIA
237–246	NORTH CAROLINA
247–251	SOUTH CAROLINA
252–260	GEORGIA
261–267	FLORIDA
268–302	OHIO
303–317	INDIANA
318–361	ILLINOIS
362–386	MICHIGAN
387–399	WISCONSIN
400–407	KENTUCKY
408–415	TENNESSEE
416–424	ALABAMA
425–428	MISSISSIPPI
429–432	ARKANSAS
433–439	LOUISIANA
440–448	OKLAHOMA
449–467	TEXAS
468–477	MINNESOTA
478–485	IOWA
486–500	MISSOURI
501–502	NORTH DAKOTA
503–504	SOUTH DAKOTA

Continued

TABLE 4.2   Continued

FIRST THREE DIGITS	STATE
505–508	NEBRASKA
509–515	KANSAS
516–517	MONTANA
518–519	IDAHO
520	WYOMING
521–524	COLORADO
525 & 585	NEW MEXICO
526–527	ARIZONA
528–529	UTAH
530	NEVADA
531–539	WASHINGTON
540–544	OREGON
545–573	CALIFORNIA
574	ALASKA
574 & 586	SOUTHEAST ASIAN REFUGEES 4/75 TO 11/79
575–576	HAWAII
577–579	DISTRICT OF COLUMBIA
580	VIRGIN ISLANDS
580–584	PUERTO RICO
585	NEW MEXICO
586	GUAM, AMERICAN SAMOA, PHILIPPINES, AND OTHER TERRITORIES
587–588	MISSISSIPPI
589–595	FLORIDA
596–599	PUERTO RICO
600–601	ARIZONA
602–626	CALIFORNIA
627–645	TEXAS
646–647	UTAH
648–649	NEW MEXICO
650–699	NOT NOW ISSUED
700–728	FORMER RAILROAD RETIREMENT, NOT NOW ISSUED
729–799	NOT NOW ISSUED

Requisite Data Entry: SSN

Date: May 07 05:08:52 AM   1997   Inquiry Number 89

PAGE 1

DATE 5-07-94   TIME 17:08:54   PPE15 V580

SSN: 123-45-6789
YOB: 1966

Mary S. Houghton
5147 -3RD STREET, APT 4, SAN FRANCISCO, CA 94105
RPTD: 9-93 TO 4-94 M
LAST SUB: 4581037

Mary S. Houghton   SSN: 123-45-6789
8383 MAIN AVE
LONG BEACH CA 90822
RPTD: 8-93
LAST SUB: 3495424

Mary S. Houghton   SSN: 123-45-6789
234 78TH AVE   YOB: 1966
LONG BEACH CA 90823
RPTD: 2-93
LAST SUB: 3549786

... AKA....
Mary S. Hough   SSN: 123-45-6789
3453 ALLEN AVE   YOB: 1966
RIVERSIDE CA 93508
RPTD: 9-92
LAST SUB: 2496762

Mary S. Hough
1654 MAIN LN
NASHVILLE TN 37864
RPTD: 8-90 TO 8-92 M
LAST SUB: 81635121

END - SOCIAL SEARCH

FORM 4.16   Social security search results might look like this.

Surname Search Example: Twenty Names

TYPICAL PRICE: (See below)

PRODUCT COMMENTS: None.

RETURN TIME: Surname Search by City $8   Immediate

                       Surname Search by State $9   Immediate

                       Surname Search by Zip $8   Immediate

Searches by Name and Date of Birth.   From entering variations of a name and a date of birth or year of birth, this search can return information on any match including address, previous address, driving license information, vehicle information, and much more.

Requisite Data Entry: Full Name

Surname Search.   Identifies address and phone number information on any last name of a subject. Search is available either by zip code, city, or state.

While this report can provide some good information, if the name is a common one then it opens a can of worms. I generally do not use these reports, as the field parameters are too large, meaning too many names are returned. In addition, the list can be bought by the first 10 names, 20 names, 50 names, 100 names, 200 names, or 500 names. You can see how excessive information can be obtained, drowning you to a point. If asked where I begin with this report, I am hard pressed to say. Really, I could use it only if I had other identifying information, such as an address, but with that information I would use a credit header—a far more efficient search tool.

Telephone Number Trace Example

TYPICAL PRICE: $6
PRODUCT COMMENTS: $1 no-hit
RETURN TIME: On-line

Telephone Number Trace.   This report is simply nothing more than a crisscross published telephone number search. For example, your telephone book has listed by name, telephone numbers; this report is listed by number, then provides a name and address if published. This report will not provide unlisted telephone numbers.

Again, this is simply a crisscross published telephone number directory. The search field here is the telephone number, and it returns the name and address affixed to this telephone number.

UCC Filings Example

TYPICAL PRICE: $23
PRODUCT COMMENTS: None.
RETURN TIME: Uniform Commercial Code Search 1–3 Days

Uniform Commercial Code Searches.   The Uniform Commercial Code Searches provide information on UCC filings from the state requested, where available. This

Requisite Data Entry: Last Name and One of Either Zip Code, City, or State
Report prepared for: MNO RESEARCH CO.

Report Type: Surname Search
    Name   Mary S. Houghton
    Zip   84637

1. Mary S. Houghton DU:DAFG Tele. (123) 456-9876 ANY STREET ADDRESS, ANYTOWN, STATE, ZIP CODE
2. Mary J. Houghton DU:DAFG Tele. (123) 456-9876 ANY STREET ADDRESS, ANYTOWN, STATE, ZIP CODE
3. Mary K. Houghton DU:DAFG Tele. (123) 456-9876 ANY STREET ADDRESS, ANYTOWN, STATE, ZIP CODE
4. Mary L. Houghton DU:DAFG Tele. (123) 456-9876 ANY STREET ADDRESS, ANYTOWN, STATE, ZIP CODE
5. Mary J. Houghton DU:DAFG Tele. (123) 456-9876 ANY STREET ADDRESS, ANYTOWN, STATE, ZIP CODE
6. Mary J. Houghton DU:DAFG Tele. (123) 456-9876 ANY STREET ADDRESS, ANYTOWN, STATE, ZIP CODE
7. Mary J. Houghton DU:DAFG Tele. (123) 456-9876 ANY STREET ADDRESS, ANYTOWN, STATE, ZIP CODE
8. Mary J. Houghton DU:DAFG Tele. (123) 456-9876 ANY STREET ADDRESS, ANYTOWN, STATE, ZIP CODE
9. Mary P. Houghton DU:DAFG Tele. (123) 456-9876 ANY STREET ADDRESS, ANYTOWN, STATE, ZIP CODE
10. Mary K. Houghton DU:DAFG Tele. (123) 456-9876 ANY STREET ADDRESS, ANYTOWN, STATE, ZIP CODE
11. Mary M. Houghton DU:DAFG Tele. (123) 456-9876 ANY STREET ADDRESS, ANYTOWN, STATE, ZIP CODE
12. Mary A. Houghton DU:DAFG Tele. (123) 456-9876 ANY STREET ADDRESS, ANYTOWN, STATE, ZIP CODE
13. Mary B. Houghton DU:DAFG Tele. (123) 456-9876 ANY STREET ADDRESS, ANYTOWN, STATE, ZIP CODE
14. Mary Y. Houghton DU:DAFG Tele. (123) 456-9876 ANY STREET ADDRESS, ANYTOWN, STATE, ZIP CODE
15. Mary Q. Houghton DU:DAFG Tele. (123) 456-9876 ANY STREET ADDRESS, ANYTOWN, STATE, ZIP CODE
16. Mary A. Houghton DU:DAFG Tele. (123) 456-9876 ANY STREET ADDRESS, ANYTOWN, STATE, ZIP CODE
17. Mary G. Houghton DU:DAFG Tele. (123) 456-9876 ANY STREET ADDRESS, ANYTOWN, STATE, ZIP CODE
18. Mary O. Houghton DU:DAFG Tele. (123) 456-9876 ANY STREET ADDRESS, ANYTOWN, STATE, ZIP CODE
19. Mary L. Houghton DU:DAFG Tele. (123) 456-9876 ANY STREET ADDRESS, ANYTOWN, STATE, ZIP CODE
20. Mary U. Houghton DU:DAFG Tele. (123) 456-9876 ANY STREET ADDRESS, ANYTOWN, STATE, ZIP CODE
21. Mary T. Houghton DU:DAFG Tele. (123) 456-9876 ANY STREET ADDRESS, ANYTOWN, STATE, ZIP CODE

END OF REPORT

FORM 4.17   Surname search results might look like this.

Requisite Data Entry: Telephone Number and Area Code

Report prepared for: MNO RESEARCH CO.
Report Type: Phone Number Trace
Number: 9999999999

ADDRESS
01. Mary S. Houghton
TEL (999) 999-9999
5147 -3RD STREET, APT 4, SAN FRANCISCO, CA 94105

END OF REPORT

FORM 4.18   Telephone number search results might look like this.

search is useful for identifying debtor addressees, business affiliations, assets, and liens of a business or individual and for assuring that assets are not subject to any prior liens.

Requisite Data Entry: Debtor Name and State or Secured Party Name and State

This report in some states has been broken up into individual reports, but here the Uniform Commercial Code (UCC) will list business, corporate, civil, and property filings for a search field of a name. This search is really one of the better ones and provides a lot of information quickly in one-stop shopping. This search is best for asset search, though, and can do little, most times, in locating people.

Requisite Data Entry: Individual Name

Report prepared for: MNO RESEARCH CO.

Report Type: UNIFORM COMMERCIAL CODE SEARCHES
Subject: Mary S. Houghton

Debtor: Mary S. Houghton
Street: 5147 -3RD STREET, APT 4, SAN FRANCISCO, CA 94105
Secured: NORPLY LEASING INC
File: 0775062 D: Seq: S: COD: T   Cart: Fl: Page: 76

Debtor: Mary S. Houghton Street: 5147 -3RD STREET, APT 4, SAN FRANCISCO, CA 94105
Secured: CALIFORNIA MORT & LOAN
File: 0785629 D: Sequence: S: COD: T   Cart: Fl: Page:76

END OF REPORT

FORM 4.19   UCC search results might look like this.

Requisite Data Entry: Vehicle Identification Number (VIN), State

RE: VEHICLES REGISTERED TO:
NAME: Mary S. Houghton
ADDRESS: 5147 -3RD STREET, APT 4, SAN FRANCISCO, CA 94105

VEHICLE1:   1985 CHEVY CAVALIER
LIC#:   46MSE93
VIN#:   1CV2MED21DY198526   EXPIRES: NOV 97

VEHICLE2:   1996 MERCEDES 280E
LIC#:   90PKDD78
VIN#:   671HL34503M24L434   EXPIRES: JUN 97

END OF REPORT

FORM 4.20   Vehicle registration search results might look like this.

Vehicle Registration Record Example

TYPICAL PRICE: $12

PRODUCT COMMENTS: None.

RETURN TIME: Vehicle Registration Record Search 1–2 days.

Vehicle Identification Numbers.   Just enter a motor vehicle identification number and registration information will be supplied. This is excellent for car repossession work when tracing cars from state to state.

With Mary's vehicle ownership record we had her name and address, so the search was conducted on that basis. We see that Mary owns two vehicles, listed in her name. This will not account for vehicles registered in someone else's name that Mary is driving. With this report we also see the registration expiration dates as well.

Worker's Compensation Report Example

TYPICAL PRICE: (See Table 4.3 below)

PRODUCT COMMENTS: None.

RETURN TIME: (See Table 4.3 below)

Worker's Compensation Claim Search.   Determines any claims or types of claims filed, employer, date of claim, and other information.

As you can see, this missing persons investigation can turn into almost any other type of investigation. Worker's compensation records by state are obviously for business

TABLE 4.3   Price and response time by state.

STATE	PRICE	RESPONSE TIME
ALASKA (AK)	18.00	1 Week
ALABAMA (AL)	18.00	1–5 Days
ARKANSAS (AR)	18.00	1–5 Days
ARIZONA (AZ)	18.00	1–5 Days
CALIFORNIA (CA)	N/A	N/A
COLORADO (CO)	18.00	1–5 Days
CONNECTICUT (CT)	18.00	1–5 Days
DISTRICT OF COLUMBIA (DC)	N/A	N/A
DELAWARE (DE)	18.00	1–5 Days
FLORIDA (FL)	16.00	1–5 Days
GEORGIA (GA)	N/A	N/A
HAWAII (HI)	16.00	1–5 Weeks
IOWA (IA)	18.00	1–5 Days
IDAHO (ID)	18.00	1 Week
ILLINOIS (IL)	18.00	1–5 Days
INDIANA (IN)	18.00	1–5 Days
KANSAS (KS)	18.00	1–5 Days
KENTUCKY (KY)	18.00	1–5 Days
LOUISIANA (LA)	18.00	1–5 Days
MASSACHUSETTS (MA)	18.00	1–5 Days
MARYLAND (MD)	18.00	1–5 Days
MAINE (ME)	18.00	1–5 Days
MICHIGAN (MI)	18.00	1–5 Weeks
MINNESOTA (MN)	18.00	1–5 Weeks
MISSOURI (MO)	18.00	1–5 Weeks
MISSISSIPPI (MS)	N/A	N/A
MONTANA (MT)	18.00	1–4 Weeks
NORTH CAROLINA (NC)	N/A	N/A
NORTH DAKOTA (ND)	18.00	1–5 Days
NEBRASKA (NE)	18.00	1–5 Days
NEW HAMPSHIRE (NH)	18.00	1–3 Weeks
NEW JERSEY (NJ)	N/A	N/A
NEW MEXICO (NM)	18.00	1–5 Days
NEVADA (NV)	18.00	1–4 Weeks
NEW YORK (NY)	N/A	N/A
OHIO (OH)	18.00	1–5 Days

TABLE 4.3   Continued

STATE	PRICE	RESPONSE TIME
OKLAHOMA (OK)	18.00	1–5 Days
OREGON (OR)	18.00	1–4 Days
PENNSYLVANIA (PA)	N/A	N/A
RHODE ISLAND (RI)	18.00	1–4 Days
SOUTH CAROLINA (SC)	18.00	1–4 Weeks
SOUTH DAKOTA (SD)	N/A	N/A
TENNESSEE (TN)	N/A	N/A
TEXAS (TX)	18.00	1–4 Days
UTAH (UT)	35.00	1–4 Days
VIRGINIA (VA)	15.00	1–4 Weeks
VERMONT (VT)	18.00	1–4 Weeks
WASHINGTON (WA)	N/A	N/A
WISCONSIN (WI)	N/A	N/A
WEST VIRGINIA (WV)	18.00	1–4 Days
WYOMING (WY)	18.00	1–4 Days

purposes, and most states understand that businesses need these records in the normal conduct of business.

When considering someone for employment, this search is important. Each state has rules and regulations on worker compensation limits of liability and reporting. This report will provide filings by name within one given state.

Requisite Data Entry: Varies by State

STATE CHECKED: CALIFORNIA
RECORDS CHECKED: 1974 TO PRESENT
DATE CHECKED: 10-04-93
CHECKED BY: JR
EMPLOYEE NAME: Mary S. Houghton
SOCIAL SECURITY: 123-45-6789

	EMPLOYEE	INJURY	TIME LOSS	COMMENTS
02/17/87	ABC DAIRY	HAND	14 DAYS	
10/25/91	JOES SHOP	KNEE	NO	
03/22/92	AAD CORP	FOOT	3 DAYS	

END OF REPORT

FORM 4.21   Worker's compensation search results might look like this.

SUPER SEARCH PRODUCTS

Within the last few years, new private on-line information brokers have developed a few new products, and more are coming along all the time. I have coined the phrase "Super Search" products to describe these searches that are revolutionary within the information brokerage industry.

In the above standard searches, a request or inquiry is made of the information broker's data bank system with a field parameter that limits the search, in most cases, to one state or county. This system has evolved in the absence of the integration of state or county limitations into "Super Data Banks." However, with the cross-linking and combining of these data banks into one data bank, one can conduct a Super Search that will search numerous states, given one field parameter. For example, a field parameter of a driver's record for Delaware would need a name and date of birth. The standard data bank would search all uploaded Delaware drivers' records and produce the output record, matching the name and date of birth requested. With Super Searches, given a field parameter of name and date of birth, Delaware drivers' records can be searched simultaneously with the drivers' records of Colorado, Florida, Iowa, Illinois, Kentucky, Louisiana, Maryland, Maine, Michigan, Minnesota, Missouri, New Hampshire, Ohio, Oregon, South Carolina, Texas, Wisconsin, and Wyoming! This is made possible because of the linking of drivers' records into one single data bank. The cost for this drivers' record Super Search is $15! The standard Delaware search is approximately $13, so for only two more dollars you get nineteen states in all.

Super Searches are not limited to drivers' records. The category includes vehicle searches, which can be searched by name, license number, vehicle identification number (VIN), or address. This search includes twenty-one states and costs approximately $15. A real estate Super Search requires inputting a name or address and will search thirty-seven states for $15! For this price the report will provide information on the address, parcel number, and other information. Note that not all counties within a given state are covered. The reason for this is that not all counties have available electronic data, either uploaded on purchasable tape by the county government itself or by information collectors (small firms that specialize in inputting information). Other Super Searches are emerging all the time, adding new states or counties to data banks.

Where do you find these Super Searches? Good question. Information brokers are coming up with new products all the time. Included in my information broker list in Chapter 8 are those companies that provide some of these products. Not all companies provide the same products; each company has different Super Search products, but generally the standard searches are somewhat similar. Companies specialize, too, and thus the product list will remain unique.

One outstanding Super Search product I want you to know about is a super credit-header search. This product, provided in different forms by various companies, is a terrific resource. What it is, simply, is the convergence of credit headers, publishers' data banks, and other business information into a super address-update. One product that has provided me with outstanding results is called *Name Shark II*. I assure you, I have no commercial interest in this product. But I can say objectively that when other products have led me to a dead-end, I inevitably resort to this excellent resource. *Name Shark II* is able

---

YOUR INFORMATION SOURCE
THE SUPER SERACH !

FOR: MNO Company   DATE: 30/09/97

INPUT CRITERIA

Last Name: KOSLOSKE
First Name: Kelli
Middle Initial: J
Date of birth:
Age Range:
City:
State: CA
Nationality:

OUTPUT
01 - RECORD MATCHING YOUR INQUIRY

Name: KOSLOSKE, KELLI J
Address: 123 California Street
City: FRESNO

State/Zip: CA 93718
Telephone Number:
Social Security Number: UNKNOWN
Date of birth: 12-10-1961
Drivers License: UNKNOWN
Sex: F
Race: UNKNOWN
Height: UNKNOWN
Weight: UNKNOWN
Validated: 1996
Other Data:
         Other address: 8754 N GREEN STREET STE 210 FRESNO CA
         Other telephone number: 818-838-9393

END OF REPORT

FORM 4.22   Typical "Super Search" surname name and address update output report.

to access records on more than 150 million people, with over 300 million records, and produces results from up to 30 years ago. The product can provide huge amounts of information, such as address, date of birth, social security number, phone number, driver's license number, state of driver's license issue, physical description, employer, employer's telephone number, and a range of other information in the file. The cost for this product is $35, and it can be run by first name and date of birth, or first name and last name, or first name, last name, and date of birth. The output report will provide all information on the first two matches. If more matches exist, then you can select others for only around $13 more per record. The limitation in using this product is that you must know enough about the person to provide a sufficient field parameter (full name and date of birth) so that the output report is limited to reasonable matches.

It is critical to mention that in the above report not all data was on file for the subject. As can be seen here, different data banks have different information, and no two data banks are exactly the same. I like this product for the multiple fields and up-to-date information produced. I have used this report from time to time when standard reports produce inadequate results. I would say that this product can be substituted for some standard products.

Chapter 5

Missing Persons Probability Analysis

Do your homework before beginning a search. This section is the first documented probability analysis applied to investigations. With the use of information in this section, you will be able to quantify the likelihood of reaching your search goals by the use of alpha (alphabetic) surname searches, or Super Search products. Based on numerical probabilities, we can predict with considerable accuracy the successful completion of searches based on the best information possible. In past years, investigators could only guess when to use a search product. Now, with the methodology explained in this chapter, you can predict success based on the U.S. Census Bureau's 1990 census demographics and population profiles and decide whether to use a credit header or a surname search. In short, we now can predict the success of low-cost search products, making your search quicker, more efficient, and less costly. In addition, this formula can tell us when a search product will produce reasonable and manageable results.

First, become familiar with the methods described below. Generally it doesn't take me more than fifteen to twenty minutes to calculate this formula, as long has I have all the information on hand and accessible whenever I need it. For the experienced investigator, this formula will be quickly grasped and can help reduce search costs and time. For the novice, this section will give you experience in calculating the potential for success and possibly give you confidence to apply a certain product to a given search.

This analysis is made possible by a U.S. Census Bureau interactive data bank, called the "Frequency Occurring Names in the U.S.," at http://www.census.gov/genealogy/www/namesearch.html. This database has been in existence only since July 1995.

This database can predict the frequency of first names by sex and last names within the United States based on census data on first names, last names, sex, race, and age. The summary information base has been collected from 377,000 persons living in 165,000 homes in 5,300 clusters or blocks, chosen with a demographic inclusion containing 7.2 million. These data provide the basis for the three name-searchable fields at http://www.census.gov/genealogy/www/namesearch.html.

I would caution privacy skeptics that this data bank contains no individual responses to the census. The Census Bureau maintains confidentiality on all persons. However, demand for surname research is satisfied by a generalized frequency of names-by-sex information base.

Before beginning, I should point out some limitations inherent in this database. Hyphenated first and last names, such as Smith-Jones, are converted to base names fields and simplified to Smith or Jones. This provides for a restriction on last names combined through marriage, and the hyphenated name cannot be predicted in frequency. In the case of double first names, such as Mary Joe, only Mary will be reflected in the data bank.

Another restriction is that John James can be read also as James John and sound accurate. In this case the name was not inverted, based on a probabilities formula. However, the name James Patricia sounded suspect, so the name would probably have been inverted to read Patricia James as correlated to a female response. Lastly, single letter names, such as S H Houghton, are not searched. In the case where a name ends in a letter, such as Alfred O, the last name is also not added to the collection.

Out of the 7.2 million sample, inadequate responses reduced the readable sample to 6.3 million. The elimination of unique names has restricted the total to 90 percent of the sampled population. Ultimately, the condensed data sample contains 88,799 unique last names; 4,275 unique female first names; and 1,219 unique male first names. African-American and Hispanic-Americans were intentionally over-sampled, according to the Census Bureau, so the frequency ratio of these communities might provide for higher proportional results. Although this database has its detractors, this is the first such sampling done by the Census Bureau, and no doubt it will get better with time and prove more accurate in years to come.

The goal here is to best express the frequency with which a name appears within the United States. Numerous first name and surname searches exist within the information broker's product line. So if we can predict frequency efficiently, then our searches will be more exact and cost less.

Census Bureau
SEARCH NAMES FILES
Pick a names file to search:
last name
female
male
Enter name(s) to search for (space delimited, case insensitive):

Start search when ready
Learn more about the name files methodology.
Send questions, comments and suggestions to: *Genealogy@Census.GOV.*
Source: U.S. Census Bureau
Last Revised: Thursday, 10-Oct-96 12:13:46
Genealogy   Census Home   Subjects A-Z

FORM 5.1 A name search form might look like this.

Input data, or the field parameter, is confined to searching last name, female first name, or male first name. You can search multiple names simultaneously, meaning you can input numerous names and the results will produce frequency rates on all name input, even if these names have no relationship to the real person's name you are seeking. As you can see from Form 5.1, only three fields can be searched. This form is simple to use. After inputting an inquiry, click on the search icon. You will have an unsecured warning window materialize, simply click on "Continue." Your results will be produced within moments. Speed for the return of results depends on your Internet Service Provider (ISP) server speed, your modem speed, and the U.S. Census Bureau's server load.

Search results need to be analyzed for application to the information broker's search products. What our analysis will produce is a formula for forecasting successful results. If the name is unusual, meaning it does not demonstrate a quantifiable number, then our chances for alpha name or surname searches might produce more efficient results than that of a common name.

To apply this to the U.S. population, the formula would be:

Total U.S. population (projection) X percent of frequency = total U.S. population with last name

For the formula to equate properly, we need qualified U.S. population statistics; the source of accurate data is the U.S. Census Bureau. The latest total U.S. population (POP-Clock) is: 266,166,207 (Form 5.2).

Census Bureau

National Clock

POPClock Projection

According to the U.S. Bureau of the Census, the resident population of the United States, projected to 11/23/96 at 6:44:22 PM is

266,166,207

COMPONENT SETTINGS

One birth every .... 8 seconds.
One death every ....14 seconds.
One international migrant (net) every ....42 seconds.
One Federal U.S. citizen (net) returning every ....108 seconds.
Net gain of one person every ....14 seconds.

Documentation for these projections.

Image not loaded

Source: U.S. Census Bureau

Please email comments (Please include your telephone number) to: pop@census.gov

Census Home   Subjects A-Z   Population Topics

FORM 5.2 POPClock.

Search results will produce the name or names searched, a percentage of frequency, a cumulative frequency, and a rank. In our search sample, our first search name of BARON has a percentage of frequency sampled of 0.006, a cumulative (total number respondents) frequency sampled of 53.380, and places 2,239th in ranking, meaning that 2,238 last names are more frequent than BARON. The searched name of CARTER has a percentage of frequency of 0.162, a cumulative frequency of 12.239, and ranks number 40 in frequency or popularity of last name. Skipping Chen, our next name of DAMRONG provides an interesting profile that can be used for our benefit in searching last names through other various data banks. DAMRONG produces a "Shucks! Not found" message. From our standpoint, this is good, since the frequency is not quantifiable. From our probability analysis, uncommon names provide more opportunities to search more various information products, with a relative success ratio higher than that of the common names of BARON or CARTER. Coco Chanel once said about fashion that "less is more," and in this model, the inverse rule applies!

Form 5.3 provides some typical search results from Census Bureau data bank.

Census Bureau

Names Search Results (last)

NAME	%freq	cum.freq	rank
BARON	0.006	53.380	2239
CARTER	0.162	12.239	40
CHEN	0.016	39.453	720
DAMRONG	shucks! not found . . .		
GALLAS	shucks! not found . . .		
GOULD	0.015	40.929	815
LAWLOR	0.002	66.278	6480
LOBODOVSHY	shucks! not found . . .		
MOLINE	0.001	68.718	8036
NOLAN	0.016	39.793	741
ROSER	0.001	74.545	13935
SHAPIRO	shucks! not found . . .		
VANDENBERG	0.002	66.242	6460
WHITE	0.279	6.834	14
WILLIAMS	0.699	2.515	3
ZIMMERMANN	0.002	64.287	5467
ZYKIN	shucks! not found . . .		

The last names file contains 88,799 names.

Source: U.S. Census Bureau

Send questions, comments and suggestions to: *Genealogy@Census.GOV.*

Back to Search   Genealogy   Census Home   Subjects A-Z

FORM 5.3   Typical search results from Census Bureau data bank.

To apply the formula,

Total U.S. population (projection) X percent of frequency = total U.S. population with last name

In the case of the name BARON, 266,166,207 x .006 (BARON) = 15,969.97242 theorem matches in the U.S. What this tells us is simply that if we run an alpha or surname search, we can expect 15,969.97242 potential matches, too much for us to fathom or interpret. We would be analyzing this report for years! Other names formulated would produce the results shown in Table 5.1.

But wait a minute, we cannot be searching 39,924.93105 persons with last name of Gould! We could be synthesizing results until the day we are too old to care anymore. So let us add more field parameters on the back end of this formula. We know the U.S. Census *Frequency Occurring in the U.S.* data bank cannot be changed, so let us change the search numbers by adding population projections by sex and age! Let us try this based on U.S. Census tables (http://www.census.gov/population/estimate-extract/nation/intfile2-1.txt). See Table 5.2.

By adding new field parameters of sex and age, look at the difference in the numbers! (Table 5.3).

TABLE 5.1   Sample name search results.

LAST NAME	FREQUENCY PERCENT	U.S. POPULATION	TOTAL SUBJECTS
CARTER	0.162%	266,166,207	431,189.25534
CHEN	0.016%	266,166,207	42,586.59312
DAMRONG	shucks! not found . . .	266,166,207	0
GALLAS	shucks! not found . . .	266,166,207	0
GOULD	0.015%	266,166,207	39,924.93105
LAWLOR	0.002%	266,166,207	5,323.32414
LOBODOVSHY	shucks! not found . . .	266,166,207	0
MOLINE	0.001%	266,166,207	2,661.66207
NOLAN	0.016%	266,166,207	42,586.59312
ROSER	0.001%	266,166,207	2,661.66207
SHAPIRO	shucks! not found . . .	266,166,207	0
VANDENBERG	0.002%	266,166,207	5,323.32414
WHITE	0.279%	266,166,207	742,603.71753
WILLIAMS	0.699%	266,166,207	1,860,501.78693
ZIMMERMANN	0.002%	266,166,207	5,323.32414
ZYKIN	shucks! not found . . .	266,166,207	0

TABLE 5.2   Resident Population of the United States: Estimates by Age and Sex, September 1, 1996 (Numbers in thousands. Consistent with the 1990 census as enumerated.)

	FEMALES	MALES
Population, all ages	135,861	129,758
Median age	35.8	33.5
Mean age	37.2	34.6
Under 5 years	9,459	9,919
5 to 9 years	9,574	10,045
10 to 14 years	9,326	9,787
15 to 19 years	9,093	9,570
20 to 24 years	8,520	8,806
25 to 29 years	9,492	9,520
30 to 34 years	10,666	10,595
35 to 39 years	11,299	11,206
40 to 44 years	10,555	10,322
45 to 49 years	9,409	9,065
50 to 54 years	7,247	6,844
55 to 59 years	5,931	5,472
60 to 64 years	5,284	4,711
65 to 69 years	5,377	4,503
70 to 74 years	4,960	3,817
75 to 79 years	4,070	2,838
80 to 84 years	2,903	1,674
85 to 89 years	1,657	737
90 to 94 years	762	256
95 to 99 years	228	60
100 years and over	48	10

To go on further, let us check out the frequency of first names. Form 5.4 shows a female first name search result for the U.S. Census Bureau's *Frequency Occurring in the U.S.* data bank. What we find here is the potential to limit searches, not on this data bank, but on private information broker's data banks, to improve our chances of a successful match.

TABLE 5.3 Adding new field parameters can change the results of a search.

LAST NAME	AGE	SEX	FREQUENCY PERCENT	POPULATION SEX/AGE CATEGORY	TOTAL SUBJECT POSSIBILITIES
CARTER	43	M	0.162%	10,322,000	16,722
CHEN	17	F	0.016%	9,093,000	1,454.88
DAMRONG	76	F	shucks! not found . . .	4,070,000	0
GALLAS	45	M	shucks! not found . . .	10,322,000	0
GOULD	51	M	0.015%	6,844,000	1,026.6
LAWLOR	34	F	0.002%	10,666,000	213.32
LOBODOVSHY	38	F	shucks! not found . . .	11,299,000	0
MOLINE	12	M	0.001%	9,787,000	97.87
NOLAN	98	F	0.016%	228,000	36.48
ROSER	56	F	0.001%	5,931,000	59.31
SHAPIRO	61	F	shucks! not found . . .	5,284	0
VANDENBERG	59	M	0.002%	5,472,000	109.44
WHITE	41	F	0.279%	10,555,000	29,448.45
WILLIAMS	21	M	0.699%	8,806,000	61,553.94
ZIMMERMANN	63	M	0.002%	4,711,000	94.22
ZYKIN	24	F	shucks! not found . . .	8,520,000	0

Census Bureau

Names Search Results (female)

NAME	%freq	cum.freq	rank
CELIA	shucks! not found . . .		
FRANCES	0.039	70.983	393
JOAN	0.306	33.795	62
JOYCE	0.364	29.505	49
MARCELLA	0.037	71.671	411
MARY	2.629	2.629	1
STEFANIE	0.021	76.694	597
SUSANNE	0.020	76.875	606
VIRGINIA	0.430	24.044	35

The female names file contains 4,275 names.

Source: U.S. Census Bureau

Send questions, comments and suggestions to: *Genealogy@Census.GOV.*

Back to Search   Genealogy   Census Home   Subjects A-Z

FORM 5.4 Female first name search result for the U.S. Census Bureau's *Frequency Occurring in the U.S.* data bank.

The numbers applied and the formula changes for females, since females are not representative of the total population. The formula now is:

Total U.S. female population (projection) X percent of frequency = total U.S. female population with first name

In this case U.S. Census Bureau female population projections place the number on September 1, 1996 at 135,861 found at http://www.census.gov/population/estimate-extract/nation/intfile2-1.txt. See Table 5-.4.

Form 5.5 shows a male first name search result for the U.S. Census Bureau's *Frequency Occurring in the U.S.* data bank.

Here again, the numbers applied and the formula changes for males, since males are not representative of the total population. The formula now is:

Total U.S. male population (projection) X percent of frequency = total U.S. male population with first name

In this case, the U.S. Census Bureau male population projections place the number on September 1, 1996 at 135,861, found at http://www.census.gov/population/estimate-extract/nation/intfile2-1.txt. See Table 5.5.

The next step is to slice the number again, as we can, by limiting the search fields to state. By this we can predict population profiles based on name, sex, age, and location. Although this system is not exact, our chances of finding someone in the thousands is not as good as someone in the tens of subject profiles. When our subject is in the tens, our search can produce quick and less costly inquiries with established search products.

Here, for example, we suspect our subject lives in Pennsylvania. Form 5.6 shows a more detailed analysis of the state in U.S. Census data found at Pennsylvania State http://www.hbg.psu.edu:80/psdc/data/.

TABLE 5.4   Female first name search results.

FIRST NAME	AGE/SEX	FREQUENCY PERCENT	POPULATION AGE	RESULTS
CELIA	NA/F	shucks! not found . . .	NA	NA
FRANCES	43/F	0.039%	10,555,000	4,116.45
JOAN	21/F	0.306%	8,520,000	26,071.2
JOYCE	26/F	0.364%	9,492,000	34,550.88
MARCELLA	30/F	0.037%	10,666,000	3,946.42
MARY	68/F	2.629%	5,284,000	138,916.36
STEFANIE	52/F	0.021%	7,247,000	1,521.87
SUSANNE	31/F	0.020%	10,666,000	2,133.2
VIRGINIA	74/F	0.430%	4,960,000	21,328

Census Bureau

Names Search Results (male)

NAME	%freq cum.freq	rank
ALEX	0.115 68.120	156
CHARLES	1.523 20.401	8
FRANK	0.581 39.169	31
GREGG	0.029 82.032	392
JAMES	3.318 3.318	1
LUIS	0.189 60.289	104
NORTON	shucks! not found . . .	
ROOSEVELT	0.028 82.201	398
SEAN	0.197 58.368	94
TODD	0.213 57.155	88
ZELMO	shucks! not found . . .	

The male names file contains 1,219 names.

Source: U.S. Census Bureau

Send questions, comments and suggestions to: *Genealogy@Census.GOV.*

Back to Search   Genealogy   Census Home   Subjects A-Z

FORM 5.5   Male first name search result for the U.S. Census Bureau's *Frequency Occurring in the U.S.* data bank.

By adding new field parameters, the chart will look this way, and look at the difference in the numbers! Knowing that the subject is single, we can add in additional field parameters, such as male householder, no wife present. You can see that the variations are limited only to your data available. See Table 5.6.

TABLE 5.5   Male first name search results.

FIRST NAME	AGE/SEX	FREQUENCY PERCENT	POPULATION AGE	RESULTS
ALEX	21/M	0.115	8,806,000	1,012,690
CHARLES	58/M	1.523	5,472,000	8,333,856
FRANK	61/M	0.581	4,711	2,737
GREGG	71/M	0.029	3,817,000	110,693
JAMES	37/M	3.318	11,206,000	37,181,508
LUIS	42/M	0.189	10,322,000	1,950,858
NORTON	48/M	shucks! not found . . .	9,065,000	0
ROOSEVELT	27/M	0.028	9,520,000	266,560
SEAN	26/M	0.197	9,520,000	1,875,440
TODD	49/M	0.213	9,065,000	1,930,845
ZELMO	59/M	shucks! not found . . .	5,472,000	0

POPULATION CHARACTERISTICS PENNSYLVANIA 1990

POPULATION

Total	11,881,643
Male	5,693,222
Female	6,188,421

AGE BY GENDER
(All Persons)

Males:

Under 18 years	1,434,311
18 to 24 years	604,706
25 to 44 years	1,804,442
45 to 64 years	1,131,938
65 years and over	717,825

Females:

Under 18 years	1,362,631
18 to 24 years	607,063
25 to 44 years	1,852,938
45 to 64 years	1,253,903
65 years and over	1,111,886

HOUSEHOLD TYPE AND PRESENCE AND AGE OF CHILDREN

Married-couple family:

With own children under 18 years	1,112,522
No own children under 18 years	1,434,864

Male householder, no wife present:

With own children under 18 years	51,934
No own children under 18 years	85,061

Female householder, no husband present:

With own children under 18 years	238,716
No own children under 18 years	253,354
Non-family households	1,316,507

EDUCATIONAL ATTAINMENT
(Persons age 25 and older)

Less than 9th grade	741,167
9th to 12th grade, no diploma	1,253,111
High school graduate (includes equivalency)	3,035,080
Some college, no degree	1,017,897
Associate degree	412,931
Bachelor's degree	890,660
Graduate or professional degree	522,086

SEX BY EMPLOYMENT STATUS
(Persons age 16 and older)

Male:
In labor force:

In Armed Forces	16,659
Civilian:	
Employed	2,952,871
Unemployed	198,697
Not in labor force	1,248,442

Female:
In labor force:

In Armed Forces	1,951
Civilian:	
Employed	2,481,661
Unemployed	146,098
Not in labor force	2,346,437

FORM 5.6   Detailed analysis of U.S. Census data for Pennsylvania.

TABLE 5.6   Variations are limited only to your data available.

LAST NAME	AGE	SEX	FREQUENCY PERCENT	PENNSYLVANIA POPULATION SEX/AGE CATEGORY	TOTAL SUBJECT POSSIBILITIES
CARTER	43	M	0.162%	1,804,442	2,923
CHEN	17	F	0.016%	1,362,631	218
DAMRONG	76	F	shucks! not found . . .	1,111,886	0
GALLAS	45	M	shucks! not found . . .	1,131,938	0
GOULD	51	M	0.015%	1,131,938	170
LAWLOR	34	F	0.002%	1,852,938	37
LOBODOVSHY	38	F	shucks! not found . . .	1,852,938	0
MOLINE	12	M	0.001%	1,434,311	14
NOLAN	98	F	0.016%	1,111,886	178
ROSER	56	F	0.001%	1,253,903	13
SHAPIRO	61	F	shucks! not found . . .	1,253,903	0
VANDENBERG	59	M	0.002%	1,131,938	23
WHITE	41	F	0.279%	1,852,938	5,170
WILLIAMS	21	M	0.699%	607,063	4,243
ZIMMERMANN	63	M	0.002%	1,131,938	23
ZYKIN	24	F	shucks! not found . . .	607,063	0

Whatever way you cut it, census data of this kind can produce revealing information. In the case of Ms. Roser, female, 98 years old, our inquiry reveals that the frequency of the Roser name, in female and age populations, would produce around 178 names. This would mean our examination of surnames searches might need to include 200 names in the list to ensure we would acquire the correct information on the subject. So a surname search might not be reasonable in this case. We might want to use other products, integrating other fields of information to locate this person.

In the case of Ms. 24-year-old Zykin, the "Shucks! Not found" message indicates that less than 1/1000th of a percent might possess this name. In the case of 607,063 potential population matches by age and sex, this would mean something in the range, at most, of five or so 24-year-old Ms. Zykins living in Pennsylvania. Although this is not an exact science, this formula can lead us to believe that the depth of the search would need to include around 10 names or fewer.

Mr. Carter, as stated above, with 2,923 potential matches would be too broad for a simple surname search, even with approximate age or date of birth added into our field parameter. Unless we could include other fields, such as first name, last known address, and so forth, this search is bound to produce too many names. In this case, we would want to try a search that would produce more limited information, and we would want to continue to develop information that could serve as the basis for a credit-header request (social security number, or name and last known address).

Chapter 6

Adoption Searches

The search for birth-parents is a natural process for making the circle of life whole or complete. I feel quite emotional whenever I take a case like this since I have two wonderful parents who have supported me constructively throughout my life. Many adoptive parents, of course, provide wonderful, loving support to their adopted children—often better than could their birth-parents. But not knowing the circumstances of being given up for adoption is often troubling for adopted children. By completing a search for their birth-parents, adopted children can explore and resolve this issue, often with surprisingly positive results.

Another reason for covering this topic is that most books or publications on the subject of investigations do not address this issue at all. I am always amazed at how level-headed my clients are who seek their birth-parents or children. Most adoptees realize that difficult and agonizing decisions were made that led to initiating the adoption in the first place. I find an unusual calm in most people who decide to undertake this type of search. Equally, I can understand that often, for medical reasons alone, one must know one's genetic lineage. It might be that the birth family has medical conditions that the adoptee needs to know about. But for whatever reason, the journey that one takes in this pursuit can be undertaken successfully.

When beginning this type of investigation, it's a good idea to get someone to help you: perhaps a friend or another family member, or maybe a spouse. It's a journey that shouldn't be undertaken alone. I believe that an objective, unemotional person is always an added plus to have on your team. Of course, this pilgrimage can be made alone, with equally promising results. But emotional support from others, along with diligence and persistence, will almost always lead to success. It's good to have someone review the investigative techniques and results. Remember the three-word investigative theory that states that all information must be "verified, verified, and verified." In a way, this is like a genealogical investigation, but we are looking only for one generation back and with fewer leads. Important clues are generally obscured due to the closed record systems that adoption confidentiality laws and regulations in the past maintained. The investigator's job here is to remove the veil of secrecy that shrouds this important relationship.

I see adoption searches as taking one of two general directions:

1. Passive investigation systems
2. Active investigation systems

The passive investigation or search is simple. Put your name on a news group, mailing list, or in the newspapers. By disseminating your message, you hope that someone with information will read it and respond. This reminds me of the space probe Voyager. I remember that tape recordings, symbols, and photographs were sent on-board the probe in hopes that some alien life form would happen upon it. Space is a pretty tough territory to cover, of course, and passive systems used in this instance are the only practical approach. But in an adoption search I would not spend too much time using them. Why sit around and wait? Maybe our subject does not know they are a subject, and maybe they are not looking. I recommend passive systems only if they are free, since the realistic chance of success is small.

Active investigation approaches are more difficult, require some experience (I hope you are learning by reading!), and require a knowledge of governmental and business behavior and rules. Active systems offer the ability to collect information, verify this collected information, and follow up these leads. In my experience, when one approach does not work, I simply change direction in mid-search and use another approach. What we need is a clearer understanding of how governments maintain and process records and a better knowledge of what information is available.

The fact is that governmental activities, such as adoptions, are subject to legal documentation and announcement. Such documentation and announcements can come in many forms. Documentation is easy to understand, and this is where most people search for information. But announcements represent a different category altogether. Legal actions are sometimes announced in local legal newspapers. This is an excellent place to start, especially in the case of an amended birth certificate (Form 6.1). Business also has systems for mandating, collecting, and maintaining forms, even when a company has gone out of business! You see, all businesses must maintain tax and employee records. These records are a great source of information, even if the information is decades old.

Unveiling the circumstances of birth and the lineage that one shares with birth-parents or children uses every technique in this book. Here, the key to the investigation is human intelligence (HUMINT) collection. The basis for this search is critical.

If this were an original birth certificate, then a collection of information in the hometowns of your parents would be simple. Family members might still live in the area. If not, then a name update on-line search might produce results, based on old telephone books, and would probably reveal a former address. With a true and accurate birth certificate, we can begin the search in earnest (use Form 6.2). Some birth certificates, interviews, or other information will lead us to what would seem to be unusable, but nice to know, information. For me, no information is unusable and always seems to lead some place. Of course, there are times when we may not want to follow certain leads, since another lead might produce quicker results, but it is good to keep all leads in mind.

I look at adoptive searches as having four phases:

1. Background information collection phase
2. Verification of documentation phase
3. On-line search phase
4. Evaluation phase

St. Mary's Hospital
New London, Delaware.
Birth Certificate

This Certifies That

Mary J. Houghton

Was born in this hospital at 10:30 p.m. on the 6th day of March 1964.
In witness whereof, the hospital has caused this certificate to be issued and signed by its duly
authorized officer and its corporate seal affixed hereto.

Sister Millie Edwards, RN.
Weight of baby at birth 7 lb. 11 oz.
Samuel K. Doe, MD.   *Sister Helen Swartz, RN. BS.*

Code 61-9240897**

Father This document was transcribed before
James Rigby Houghton and hereby certified as signed before
Birthplace me on this 26th day of May, 1991
Smalltown, Texas 04/05/34 Under the laws of Delaware.

Mother
Sally Mary LeMonds *June A. Monroe*
Birthplace
Wedstock, Wyoming 05/02/38 Copy certified by June A. Monroe
Notary Public # 14957
Place of Marriage
Louisville, Kentucky 06/06/56

**(Check this code if amended birth certificate. This code often is the code for either the real
birth certificate or in some states it is the case code.)

FORM 6.1   Sample amended birth certificate.

The background information phase is really the difficult portion of this investigation.
We are beginning with few known research points or information. So when beginning to
search, most often we will begin with the birth certificate. Birth certificates have many
different informative elements, as seen below. Frequently, however, we must start with
a false or amended birth certificate. This means that the real birth certificate is not releasable and is sealed. Maybe the adoption happened in a state other than where the birth
occurred, and the birth certificate of the adopted individual is a *second* birth certificate,
with the adoptive parents' names and addresses, making the birth-parents and adoptive
parents naturally seem the same. This is the most difficult situation.

Asking questions of everyone who might know of the adoption and the story behind
it is a good step. Often adoptive parents are not willing to provide information, or their

	Fill in responses here
Mother's or Father's legal and proper name (full first, middle, and last names) • possible surname search • possible "Super Search" product	
Height, weight, color of hair, color eyes, family information, etc., check the systems analysis matrix	
Mother's or Father's date of birth • possible check of county criminal information or drivers check by state • "Super Search" product	
Mother's or Father's last and all known telephone numbers, from old telephone books • possible crisscross search	
Mother's or Father's Social Security number • possible "credit header" search	
Mother's or Father's former addresses (current or last known, to previous) • possible on-line credit header search if within the last seven years • "Super Search" product	
Mother's or Father's former or current employment (name, address, and telephone number) • possible telephone call to human resource department or archived records	
Mother's or Father's driver's license or automobile license • possible on-line DMV search by state	
Relatives/Friends • possible telephone call	
Mother's or Father's schools (start with most recently attended) • possible telephone call to alumni association or admissions department	
Mother's or Father's business connections • on-line business search numerous products	
Mother's or Father's State Professional licenses • on-line search/telephone call to the state's licensing bureau	
Mother's or Father's former or current military • possible contact with US Government	
Mother's or Father's association memberships • possible telephone to association	

FORM 6.2   Adoption Dossier (when you have an original birth certificate).

memories may have become clouded, but friends and relatives might provide some initial details. This would include contacting the adoption agency or attorneys involved. Approaching this part of the search calls for diplomacy. Of course, your contacts at the agency or law office really are not required to say anything, but sometimes someone with a sympathetic ear can be found. Hopefully, at least the state and city of birth can be found by asking these individuals a few questions.

If the adoption agency is unwilling to provide full disclosure, then I suggest you attempt to settle for some middle-ground information, such as a city and state of birth. This will provide a framework from which to operate. I often encounter people who will not disclose information, so I at least try to walk away with some information. Pose the question: "Oh, since I'm here, could you at least let me know where I was born?" The birth location is important, because this is where your original birth certificate more than likely resides.

If you do not have your original birth certificate but rather an amended birth certificate, I suggest that you begin searching for other records, such as a petition to adopt (from the court), the final decree of adoption (from the court), your hospital birth records, a sheet with "nonidentifying" information (from the agency or lawyer).

A passive method of attempting to acquire records would be to file a WAIVER OF CONFIDENTIALITY at the adoption agency, hospital of your birth, and state adoption bureau. Although the success of this approach might be minimal, I suggest that any and all avenues be pursued; let the system sort out what it will and will not do. Many states will release information when a waiver is signed by adoptees and a birth-parent. Some agencies will even search for the birth-parent to request that contact be arranged (e.g., Hawaii, Pennsylvania, and others). In addition, I would write a letter to the vital statistics bureau in the state where you believe you were born. Depending on the information you have, you may want to get a copy of your own amended birth certificate, your birth-mother's and birth-father's birth certificate, and so on.

You can also do a search for marriage and death certificates of your known relatives if you have their names and/or birth dates. Again, if you are working with an amended birth certificate, talking with relatives, adoptive parents, adoptive agency, lawyers, or the hospital and doctors for non-identifying birth-parent information is necessary. If you can find anything, such as a state of birth, this will put you on your way to solving the case and attempting to get an original birth certificate. What is important on this amended birth certificate is the date of birth. It provides a time frame of what may be within a few months of the original birth—maybe three or so months before.

Our goal is to determine the real name or social security number of the subject, or, in this case, the birth-parents or child. This can be done by backtracking the records currently available and following this up with a review of newspapers of the approximate date of birth. Frequently, the names of the real birth-parents will be published as a legal notice. This search step is undertaken in the city where the birth date is recorded on the currently available documentation. The search should encompass several weeks before that date. I like to search the legal and major newspapers first, the secondary or smaller newspapers next. If the adoption was many years ago, say 40 or 50 years, archived records at the county recorder's office might also prove useful, just as in genealogy searches. But the county recorder's office of the county of birth and of the adoption, if they are the same, might demonstrate other leads such as a real birth certificate.

Birth mother's and father's name, address, date of birth, Social Security number, time of your birth, place and location of your birth is our goal at a minimum.	mother's name_____ mother's place of birth_____ mother's date of birth_____ father's name_____ father's place of birth_____ father's date of birth_____
Check amended birth certificate for hospital, agency, attorneys, or other identifying information on an organization. Call the organization and seek additional information, such as place of birth. A location is needed to back-trace for an original birth certificate.	*Fill in answers here*
Talk with friends, neighbors, relatives, or family for all relevant information.	
Talk with foster parents for relevant information (great source of knowledge!).	
Organizations dealing with the adoption, such as hospital, agency, attorneys, etc., and list all known telephone numbers for the organizations you have contacted or might need to contact, with name of contact person (keep using the same contact person, if they are helpful, if not, call again and try to talk with someone else). Also the former employees that might have handled your case, such as former nurses, former doctors, former employees, etc.	
Check legal notice newspapers for adoption announcement in county of adoption (as seen on birth certificate).	
Check county and state records for identifying numbers to correspond with amended birth certificate codes.	
Check county and state records for duplicate birth certificates, maybe the real one (small chance here, which is why it is on bottom of this list).	

FORM 6.3   Adoption Dossier (when you do not have an original birth certificate).

The original birth certificate produces identifying information on the individual, such as name, place of birth, date of birth, place of marriage, and sometime occupation. For this reason, the original birth certificate is a key element of the search. Identifying information on the subject can be obtained from agencies, lawyers, doctors, or hospitals involved in the adoption. This information might not be as revealing as the original birth certificate, but might provide searchable field parameters. Use Form 6.3 if you do not have an original birth certificate.

This scenario might continue by searching county records for a child of your sex born within the county or adjacent county (nice to know if you were born in a hospital or not). This will produce a list of names that might identify you. A simple elimination process is then conducted. However, the list might be large, and we will need other identifying elements of your birth-parents. This will eliminate other names on this list quickly (for example, say it was a German couple!), by further limiting our search we increase chances of success.

NONIDENTIFYING INFORMATION CHECKS

In some cases, adoptees are provided with nonidentifying birth-parents information. This information does not name or provide information to identify the birth-parents. But some of this information might be used to search for the birth-parents. Now I won't tell you this would be easy, but some leads might exist. Typical birth-parent nonidentifying information might include age, occupation, level of education, race and/or ethnicity, religion, physical description, hobbies, talents, marital status, medical history, and circumstances surrounding the adoption. In some cases you might also receive the first names of the birth-parents, medical history, ages, and physical description of the extended birth-family.

It is the combination of these nonidentifying factors that might provide a profile for a search. If you know only the city or county, you might have enough to begin a search. For example, if we know that the person we are looking for, based on nonidentifying information, is a white female of German ancestry, was born in 1943, and was Catholic, single, and worked as a clerk, this might be enough to begin checking local Catholic churches for information; older church employees or priests might provide some information or leads, maybe even a name. Additionally, county records might provide a range of possibilities, including records such as civil court filings, voters registration, property records, tax assessor records, probate, and so on. Anyone matching the profile you have constructed from this list will offer contact prospects. I would have a third party do the initial contacting, if possible. This technique is speculative and offers only marginal probability of success, but in this business, cases are sometimes solved by chance. It is knowing how to develop a profile that offers the most promise—and knowing where to begin a search—that is critical here. And again, knowing a city or county offers the most solid prospect for success.

NAME SEARCHES

Name searches may be conducted based on one other identifying element: a former address from an old address book or other source of information. Below I have described a few key places to check. If all you have is a common name but no address, simply review telephone books from the era in the local library. At this point we want to establish some verifiable information. Not only might this lead us to the subject, but it will help identify the individual once we find him or her.

1. Telephone books. Libraries have in their archives or on the shelf telephone books from the local community up to forty years back, or more. At that time, most people who had a telephone were listed, and most addresses were published. If the name of the subject is unusual, I would next try a search of national on-line telephone directories or an information broker's national alpha search. As discussed earlier, for common names, you might become inundated quickly and have too many false leads. But the new Super Search products can provide real assistance. *Name Shark II,* described in Chapter 4, offers one of the best means for searching historical data banks that combine with current records.

2. Voter Records. You can also check voter registration records in the county government's archival library, extending back many years. If the subject was registered to vote, then the address, party affiliation, occupation, and other information will be available.

3. Polk Directories. The Polk directories found in libraries are available for major cities throughout the country. This directory is found in hardbound form and was one of the original crisscross directories. With a name one can find the address, or with the address one can find a name. This directory has more information than normally included in a telephone book.

4. Property records. If you know a name, check historical property records surrounding the period of the approximate birth date. If property was owned, then an address will result.

5. Tax assessments. Examine tax assessor information from that era. Similar to the property ownership records, the tax assessor records demonstrate taxes paid on property.

6. Probate Court records. If a name is found, Probate Court records of the era will reveal significant information on a person involved in probate. This is located at the probate court in each county.

7. Census records. While the census records at the county government's archival library are excellent resources, the files are protected for seventy-two years, so the subject will need to be old enough so that relevant material is available.

8. Religious records. If you know anything about your religion or baptism, contact local churches or synagogues of the area for records and information. This is especially promising if the agency that placed you was a private, religious organization. Some religious agencies in particular are known to baptize infants shortly after birth and before the adoption. You can usually get a copy of your baptismal certificate if this is the case. Churches and other religious institutions also maintain very good records and can often be useful in other ways. These records are generally available, since they are used for various purposes, including genealogy.

9. Employer records. This background phase of information research might very well include exploring employer records for leads on a birth-father or birth-mother. Some of the companies that the birth-parents worked for may be out of business, however their records are generally still available someplace. I would start with state Uniform Commercial Code archived filings, Better Business Bureau (can provide a contact name), a regional Who's Who, and so forth. Now, I am not going to tell you this technique works every time, but it is one more option in your quest. If the company is out of business, I can think of no reason why the company files could not be seen. The company files will produce a social security number, and this number, as we know, can provide updated residence information within minutes, using a credit header search. If the company is still in business, then the files may not be releasable, but they might be viewed in the company's offices.

I would make the request, and tell them the truth. Most people are willing to help under these circumstances. I recall one case where the only lead to the birth-father was his employment at a business that had ceased operations years earlier. The files were still available at the former business owner's home. In California, business sales records or tax liabilities must be maintained for four years. A simple Secretary of State's business name Uniform Commercial Code (UCC) search will produce the registered agent's name and address. I really like this technique. It is not a method always used, but it provides the social security number for an individual; and with this number, the search is concluded quickly, with a credit header update. Now, if the time frame we are searching for is beyond this four-year period (and most likely it will be), state records will be archived, but generally UCC will provide the last-known registered agent's name and address. By contacting this person, employment records might still be available. People are often "pack rats" and do keep these records. Old Better Business Bureau records might produce a contact name at the former company.

10. Press accounts. Newspaper announcements of the birth or adoption offer some possible leads. Search the local newspapers, the most likely source. Legal newspapers might have information on the adoption itself.

Once the real names and former address or social security number of the birth-parents is known, then it becomes a typical update of name and address. Then there are the common methods of searching for background data as we have discussed in earlier chapters. If you have the social security number, simply do a credit header as in any other type of investigation. The results will provide you with the updated name and address of whoever is using this social security number. This might solve the case. With some of the new Super Search products available, I would suggest that going back twenty-five to thirty years on an old address would prove informative. Although on average Americans move today every four years, in years past this was not the case, and old addresses are just as good as new ones in the information industry. Even if you have no name, it is possible to buy a list of all residents for an address twenty-five to thirty years ago, and conduct a crisscross or reverse Super Search.

So now you see how this mind-set of linking information to systems develops into solving cases quickly. Some of the systems I described are governmental, and some are the normal methods of business. What we are really talking about here is governmental and legal records analysis. By knowing the standard administrative systems that people employ, we can acquire verified, useful information quickly—and with some certainty that this will eventually lead to a case conclusion. Public records or private employer records analysis, in this case, provides a benefit and directness virtually unknown in this field. Each piece of information you might have can and will lead someplace. It is knowing what to do with leads that counts.

Most professional investigators, if they are good, will provide information within a short period of time and might even be able to solve the case within days or a couple weeks. When I search for missing persons, I generally attempt to complete the case within three days. Because these paper records are housed at government offices, libraries, and so on, a local search is mandatory in some cases. However, in the case of electronic data, I would say a national firm could easily solve the case just as quickly. When information is housed within data banks, it is easy to access this information anywhere within the United States. But remember, not all public records are in electronic media form.

If you can have a court open your adoption files for cause, such as for medical purposes, you often will have the following documents: original birth certificate, petition to adopt, final decree, reports on initial interviews with birth-parents, and birth-parents' medical history, biographical information, and signed relinquishment or consent form.

CASE EXAMPLES

The following examples represent true-to-life cases. The names are not real, to protect the innocent, and some of the details in some of the cases represent composite experiences.

Mary L. Roser Roberts

With an original birth certificate, my client provided me with enough information to begin. My search centered on Mary L. (maiden name Roser) Roberts, born 1/07/41 in Boise, Idaho, and Samuel K. Longher, born 5/29/39 also in Boise, Idaho. I checked other Rosers and Longhers in Boise, and left a message in three cases. With no returned telephone calls, I proceeded to run a Super Search product called *Name Shark II*, using field parameters of name, date of birth, and location of birth. I was able to come up with a list of former addresses, a current address, social security number, and a current telephone on both subjects. I contacted both and discovered that the birth-mother was willing to see the daughter. So I turned over the information on how my client could contact the birth-mother. Within twenty-four hours, the birth-mother had been contacted by my client, and they talked on the telephone and later meet. The birth-father had problems with my releasing this information and had not wished to be contacted. He stated that he felt guilty and had moved on with his life. I still maintain the telephone number and contact him annually. He has yet to consent to the release of his information. Case time: two days.

Janet O. Smith Baker

My client provided me with an original birth certificate that included the names, birth year only, place of marriage, and place of birth for the birth-parents. Typical telephone tracing provided no leads since the birth-mother's name was Janet O. (maiden name Smith) Baker, born in 1945, in Raleigh, North Carolina. The birth-father's name was James Baker, born in 1937, in Bakersfield, California. An exact date of marriage was provided as New York, New York on 6/05/64. After running a probability analysis, I concluded that a surname search would yield too many names to search. With no local family members identifiable, the investigation apparently had no place to go. However, voter's registration records at the county government's archival library told me the social security numbers of both Janet Baker and James Baker. By running a credit header search on both social security numbers, I discovered that the birth-mother was deceased. The birth-father was now living in Dallas, Texas. I contacted the father, and he agreed to talk with his daughter (my client). I provided my client with the information necessary to contact him. She flew for a reunion to Dallas that weekend. Both have become good friends and are happy to be reunited. Case time: six days.

Christopher L. Rupert

A client provided me with an *amended* birth certificate, dated 12/17/70. The adoption agency was the St. Mary's Adoption Agency. He knew nothing of his birth-family, and I mean *nothing*, except that his birth-father had been born in San Francisco. None of the information on the case pointed to the birth-parents. By checking the San Francisco *Chronicle*, I discovered three birth announcements for children born 12/17/70 that matched my client's race and presumed ethnic background. I discovered three matches: Steven B. Chrisholm, Bennett A. Patrie, and Alexander O. Rupert. This provided the basis for further research. By searching the names, I discovered that one of these children still lived in San Francisco; it was an uncommon name of Chrisholm, so this name was eliminated. A former address of Bennett A. Patrie was updated via an on-line search product, and he was discovered to be living in Los Angeles, California. Another one eliminated. The third name, Alexander O. Rupert, seemed to the best lead, but we needed confirmation.

By running the name, Alexander O. Rupert, with a former address of the parents, listed in the newspaper article, nothing came up. This is good evidence that the person does not exist. I checked county court records and discovered that the file on Alexander O. Rupert and his parents, Christopher L. and Rose K. Rupert of 1291 Union Street, San Francisco, California in 1970, had been sealed. This was very strong evidence that we might have a match. By running an on-line search, I discovered updated addresses on Christopher L. Rupert, the suspected birth-father; he had moved to 20362 Westwind Avenue, Las Vegas, Nevada. By contacting Christopher Rupert, I was told that, indeed, he was the father of a baby son, born in 1970, and had given the child up for adoption to the St. Mary's Adoption Agency after his wife had left him. Since he did not have enough resources to support the child and was living in Golden Gate Park during the late 1960s and early 1970s as part of the hippie generation, he had given the child up for adoption. Here was a match of adoption agencies! We were getting close now.

Christopher Rupert stated that he would like to talk with his birth son. But I needed further confirmation. I called the St. Mary's Adoption agency and told them the story and who I was. At first they stated they could provide nothing to me, but when I talked to the supervisor I told her that these people will be getting together anyway. I asked if they could at least confirm that these are the correct people involved. The supervisor saw my point and stated they were the correct people. The supervisor also gave me the social security number for the birth-mother. I contacted my client and give him the information to contact his birth-father. They talked on the telephone and agreed to meet later that month. An on-line social security trace of the birth-mother demonstrated that she had moved back home to Peoria, Illinois. I contacted the birth-mother, and she stated she would contact my client. My client called back after receiving the telephone call from the birth-mother. They had agreed to correspond via mail for the time being. Case time: four days.

Wilma E. Gallas

A client contacted me without an original birth certificate. The *amended* birth certificate had an adoption agency listed, Argos Adoptions, Inc., of Cleveland, Ohio, and attorney Ross F. McGowen, Cleveland, Ohio. The birth date was 9/14/67. The client knew that she had been born a Lutheran and had been told her baptism had been performed in Oakland, California. After contacting the pastors of the four Lutheran churches in Oakland, California, I was invited to search the church records. After searching the files of two of the churches, I discovered no baptisms for baby girls with my client's race born on or near 9/14/67. At the third church I discovered a possible match with date and race. The name produced was Clara D. Gallas. Having run the Census name-frequency matrix described earlier, I knew that this name was uncommon in the United States, ranking below 1822 other names. Only one parent had been listed on the certificate of baptism, Wilma E. Gallas. I made a copy, thanked the pastor, and left.

On my way home, I stopped by the Alameda County Recorder's Office and searched for the original birth certificate of Clara D. Gallas. I was able to identify the voter registration records of Wilma E. Gallas in 1967, and I made a copy. By running the address on the voter registration records, I discovered in the Polk Directory that the listed address in 1967—9137 Broadway, Oakland, California—had two residents: George A. Carter and Wilma E. Gallas. Checking the current telephone book produced no leads, but telephone books up to 1992 revealed that Wilma Gallas had lived at the same address on Broadway. By running an on-line address update, I discovered that Wilma Gallas had moved four years earlier to 4613 Westmont, Fremont, California, and had the telephone number (510)123-1234. I called her and gently told her my assignment. I was delighted to find her happy to learn that her baby girl had been seeking her out. I asked her if she remembered the adoption agency she had gone to, and she remembered right away that it was the Argos agency in Cleveland, a transaction arranged for by a friend of hers. A match of the adoption agency is a good sign, and as I talked to Gallas further, I determined we probably had a match.

In contacting the agency in Cleveland, I learned that they would not cooperate with my search at that time, but an official told me they would provide the information if they had signatures from both the adoptee and the birth-parent. I called my client and she agreed—and so did Gallas. I made arrangements to have WAIVER OF CONFIDEN-

TIALITY forms signed by each of them and had them sent to Cleveland by overnight delivery service. I called the agency the next day and asked if they had received the forms. The agency acknowledged receiving them, but, unfortunately, added that it would take two months to process. "Typical bureaucrats!" I thought. I immediately contacted the manager of the agency and told him the story. He agreed to release the information immediately.

I called my client and gave her the news. She was so happy she asked if she could meet her birth-mother that very day. I called Gallas and told her the same story. Learning that she did not have transportation and that she was house-bound by a work injury, I offered to pick her up and take her to San Francisco so that she and her birth-daughter could meet. She readily agreed, and three hours later, they were having dinner together and talking as if they were old friends. After talking with her birth-mother, my client decided not to seek out her birth-father. Case time: five days.

AFTER YOU HAVE FOUND SOMEONE

How one handles the connection after someone being sought is found is just as important as the search itself—actually more so—and it must be handled with great sensitivity. In most cases, the parties eventually are interested in connecting with the past. But this is not always true, and you must be prepared for the unexpected. A letter is generally a good first step, allowing the other party an opportunity to consider the offer and then to contact you at their own pace. Few formulas work, given this situation, since time, blame, family secrets, and other things are factors here. An understanding, honest, and sincere approach, devoid of accusations or ascribing guilt, is an approach often used by the parties involved at their first meeting to produce a positive outcome. What we are witnessing here is really the restoration of the circle of life. This truly can be a time of great joy.

Chapter 7

Genealogy

Reaching back to better understand our historical roots is becoming an increasing passion for many Americans. I would like to pass along a few tips that professional investigators use to efficiently resolve cases, based on my own practice. Because they are professionals, private investigators are driven to develop evidence, track down leads, and solve cases without wasting any time. Some proven techniques we employ can significantly improve the efficiency of a genealogical search. The information sources described in previous chapters apply equally to this type of search. The main difference with genealogical research is that the people we are pursuing are generally deceased, and the information sources generally consist of written documentation not found in electronic data banks. For this reason, genealogical research, most often, cannot be done from your house.

Additionally, by its very nature, genealogical research is a search that has no end! Looking for family history could theoretically be dated back to the earliest of written materials, even beyond. The study of family histories or genealogy, is a complex search—a search for information linking individuals and relationships through historical documentation. It is quite simple in theory. It is the bringing together of information from various sources to connect family lines. As a practical matter, however, the search is not easy. Massive amounts of extraneous information can be uncovered quickly in the search. And while you are at one location searching, you might find cross references that lead to more information elsewhere.

As in adoption searches for birth parents or birth children, genealogy can be conducted as a passive or active investigation. Passive systems are defined as bulletin boards, requests for information, or message postings, in the hopes that someone seeing the message will respond. An active search or investigation is the pursuit of information from various sources and bringing together reference documents to complete a mosaic to better understand relationships between resource information.

Although I respect passive approaches, I don't have a great deal of confidence that someone else will gratuitously provide information to me that will drive my search forward. Passive systems are useful only if carefully targeted: specific requests for information must be placed in the right message boards or in places where response is likely. However, because passive requests must be drawn narrowly, the realistic chances of someone being able to piece together requested information and respond are remote. For example, information pertaining to an individual living in the 1830s in New England would be hard to assemble if passive systems alone were used. Obviously, no one from that era still lives, and others with direct knowledge might not be reading the messages on the day or week when it is posted. Passive investigations have a place, but they require persistence in posting information frequently—on a weekly or monthly basis in a file, message board, or news group specifically targeted to the geographic area where we believe pertinent information resides.

Active investigative systems really yield the most promise. An active search begins with the assemblage of information from basic sources, such as family members, Bibles, old letters, church information, photographs, and so on. When pursuing this course, it is important to develop some type of written family tree or computer program that can assist in the assembly of information by placing it in an easy-to-read and organized fashion. Numerous organizers are available, and this is where I would begin.

It is difficult to discuss the beginning of this search, since what we all know about our families varies widely. Most genealogists I have met are someplace in the middle of a search, and they are concerned with sources of information more than other elements of the investigation. As in every investigation, we start with some known information. Information resources are divided into several categories, most of which overlap in one way or another:

1. **Modern on-line information sources**. These sources are represented by electronic records that produce instant information, based on a field parameter input of data. These systems, as discussed earlier, are used for business, credit, and more and more, for government. Individual end-users, you and I, must most often go through information brokers to access this information, since it comes from numerous sources and is aggregated by professional information brokers into numerous information products. Because this information is active and updated often, fees are charged for processing and storage. This information is generally available from the mid-1980s to the present.

2. **Written current to semi-current government and business documents**. This information is provided in forms that produce reproducible material. It is generally housed in local, state, and federal government offices, or in private business locations. In the case of government information, it is represented by public records and can be accessed by all individuals simply by asking. This information sometimes might be on a local area network (LAN). For example, some public records demanded here might be in the form of property ownership and tax records. Some local governments have this information dating from the mid-1970s or so to the present. This information is in active data banks, but is historical in nature, meaning it does not have bearings on current transactions.

3. **Written archived information since 1789 in the U.S. Government, churches, and business**. Of course, the Government is a pack rat. Huge amounts of archived information is squirreled away as historical documents in libraries everywhere. Here is where family histories can be pieced together, beginning from the early days of the Republic around 1789. Some information prior to 1789 is archived by the U.S. Government, but not much. Sources of information here include census, immigration, birth, death, associations, business registrations, tax, military, probate, and property. The National Archive and Records Administration (NARA) houses much of this information, as do county archived libraries at the local level. Churches are also good sources of information during this time.

4. Pre-Revolutionary Sources. Pre-Revolutionary sources of information are limited to major repositories, such as the Library of Congress and the Archives, and to university libraries and private collections. Some associations and societies have information dating from this time.

5. Foreign sources. Church, government, and town and village registration information is available to some extent here too. If the region to be searched is Europe, then record keeping is reasonably good. In England, for example, churches have logged and registered all births and deaths since the 1400s. But be prepared to do some travel.

While searching for records, it is important to develop a multi-tasking system, allowing you to search and follow up on leads instantly, as they become apparent. If one record suggests a link, then other records might also be found to help establish this link at the same location. Information of this sort most often comes in clusters. We have all heard stories of discoveries in boxes of old records at a library. Well, they do exist! I have developed a small matrix, below, to help better explain that sources of genealogical information need to be grouped by time period. We are reaching back many generations, and these periods had different collection and information storage techniques.

The key is to identify when someone needed to contact the government and register information, such as a birth, death, business activity, tax payment, property exchange, census, probate, civil and criminal court, immigration, and so forth. Remember, government sources of information allow the release of individual census identifying information from seventy-two years back. Form 7.1 is a simple matrix to assist you in clustering information.

GOVERNMENT AND PRIVATE SOURCES OF INFORMATION

National Archives and Records Administration (NARA)

The National Archives and Records Administration (NARA) may be found at (http://www.nara.gov/nara/menus/genealog.html). In general, for genealogical research, the NARA is a great place to research three main types of unique Federal Government-held records:

1. Census records (four microfilm catalogs)
    [1] 1790-1890
    [2] 1900
    [3] 1910
    [4] 1920
2. Military records (microfilm catalog)
3. Immigration and passenger records (microfilm catalog)

There is no charge for the use of records in the National Archives for genealogical research. It's free! A twenty-five-page brochure is available at the National Archive libraries that discusses genealogical research in general, and then outlines the genealogical records in the

Year Searching	Source
1980s to present	• Electronic or information broker products • Local county government public records • State government records (generally individual information needs consent of the individual) • Federal government records (generally individual information needs consent of the individual) • Business records • Religious records
1930s to 1980s	• Local county government public records (archived at the county library, individual records are available) • State government records (archived at state libraries or schools, few individual records are available) • Federal government records (archived information at such places as NARA, few individual records are available) • Business records (archived, if they exist) • Religious records (your church local and national, or LDC)
1789 - 1930s	• As above, but individual records and identifying records on persons become available from state and federal governments. Specific records here are immigration, census, military, etc.

FORM 7.1   Genealogy Sources of Information.

National Archives. It includes the information necessary to research your request. You can receive a copy by mail by contacting the office at:

Genealogy Research
Reference Services Branch
National Archives and Records Administration
8th St. and Pennsylvania Ave., NW, Room 205
Washington, DC 20408
(202) 501-5400

    or at:

Library of Congress at National Genealogy Reference
Main Reading Room
Washington, DC 20540
(202) 707-5000,
or Local History and Genealogy, (202) 707-5537.

The *Guide to Genealogical Research in the National Archives* is available for $25 and contains information about individuals whose names appear in census records, military service and pension files, ship passenger and arrival lists, land records, and many other types of records. This Guide shows how to tap this rich resource, explaining what types of records are preserved in the National Archives and what specific information about individuals is included in each type of record. It is available from the publications office by calling (202) 501-5325. For more information on genealogical research, contact the Reference Services Branch.

Free copies of the general information leaflets (GILs) and the sales brochure are available from:

Publications Distribution
National Archives, Room G9
Seventh and Pennsylvania Avenue, NW
Washington, DC 20408
(202) 501-7190 or (800) 788-6282 (fax: 301-763-6025)

The *Guide to Genealogical Research* and the microfilm catalogs are also important tools for the genealogist and may be purchased from the Publications Distribution. The texts of the microfilm catalogs and GIL No. 3 are also available on the NARA gopher. For the catalogs, go to the "Microfilm Catalogs" heading under "Genealogical Holdings." The text of GIL No. 3 is found under "Information for Archivists and Records Managers"/" Archival Information"/"Publications."

NARA Genealogical Workshops

Genealogical workshops are available through the Education Branch of the National Archives and Records Administration, 8th St. and Pennsylvania Ave., NW, Room 505, Washington, DC 20408 (202) 501-5400 or (202) 501-5525. I highly recommend attending any one of these workshops. The Education Branch staff provides some of the best training in the use of NARA archived documents available and will shorten your search time. Since the number of documents at the NARA is overwhelming, I can tell you that even veteran investigators need these workshops. Topics include: census records, ship's passenger lists, naturalization records, military service records, as well as many other genealogical topics. This is one place where you must trust the experts, otherwise you may find yourself collecting your social security checks at the NARA years later—while trying to complete your research!

While many diverse groups visit NARA's facilities nationwide and sample the agency's records, genealogists no doubt are the most numerous users of NARA's research rooms in Washington, D.C., and the thirteen regional archives. NARA, therefore, continues to make special efforts to satisfy the needs of genealogists.

NARA Genealogy Holdings

NARA offers the public many free general information leaflets (GILs) regarding its records of genealogical value. NARA distributes *Aids for Genealogical Research*, a free publications catalog that describes NARA or commercial works focusing on genealogy. This catalog, for example, briefly explains NARA's three most important genealogical holdings—census, military, and immigration and passenger records; it also describes mail-order forms and genealogy workshops and courses; and it lists NARA's thirteen regional archives. Free copies of the GILs and sales brochure are available from:

Publications Distribution (NECD)
National Archives, Room G9
Seventh and Pennsylvania Avenue, NW
Washington, DC 20408
(202) 501-7190 or (800) 788-6282 (fax: 301-763-6025)

Genealogy holdings can be found at the National Archives Building (Archives I), Pennsylvania Avenue, between Seventh and Ninth Streets, Washington, DC (inquire@ arch1.nara.gov) and at National Archives (Archives II), 8601 Adelphi Road, College Park, MD (inquire@arch2.nara.gov).

A Fax-on-Demand service, for use with the handset on a fax machine, gives information on many topics. Call (301) 713-6905. Other telephone numbers are for Public Reference Information (202) 501-5400; Center for Legislative Archives (202) 501-5350; and Genealogy Staff (202) 501-5410.

Paper-to-paper copies of most documents can be made on self-service copiers at a cost of 10¢ per page. Microfilm to paper copies are 25¢ per image.

Catalogs of Microfilm Publications is a series of catalogs describing National Archives microfilm publications related to subjects of high research interest. Each catalog is compiled through an extensive review of all microfilmed records to locate publications relevant to each topic. The catalogs contain both detailed descriptions of the records and roll-by-roll listings for each publication. Other catalogs in the series cover the following topics: American Indians, Black Studies, Diplomatic Records, Genealogical and Biographical, Research, Military Service Records, and Federal Court Records.

The Family and Military Genealogy Military Reference Branch, National Archives and Records Administration, 8th St. and Pennsylvania Ave., NW, Washington, DC 20408 (202) 501-5385 holds military service records and veterans' benefits records (pensions and bounty-land application files) for service performed from the Revolution (1775) through the early twentieth century. The NARA does not have Confederate pension records, which were authorized by some southern states. To order photocopies of military service records requires the use of National Archives Trust Fund Form 80 and separate forms are needed for each file requested. You can obtain copies of this form and additional information about military service records from the Reference Services Branch at (202) 523-3218. Your order must contain the following information: soldier's full name; period/war in which he or she served; state from which he or she served; branch of service; and whether the service was with the Union or Confederate forces.

Military records from the nineteenth century on can be found at:

Suitland Reference Branch
National Archives and Records Administration
Washington, DC 20409
(202) 763-7430

This office holds historical material, including Land Office records, military personnel records dating prior to 1900, State Department personnel overseas posting records since 1935, the Japanese war relocation records, records of the U.S. military governments of Germany and Japan, as well as records of all military actions dating from the Revolutionary War through 1963. The office provides reference assistance in locating historical material and will accept reference questions both in writing and by phone.

The Military Reference Branch maintains records of military personnel separated from the U.S. Air Force, Army, Coast Guard, Marine Corps, Navy, Confederate States, volunteers, as well as veterans records. The publication, *Military Service Records in the National Archives of the United States*, provides a detailed list of the holdings and pertinent details about the records. It is available for a small fee from the publications office at the office of Military Services Branch, National Archives and Records Administration, 8th St. and Pennsylvania Ave., NW, Room 13W, Washington, DC 20408, (202) 501-5385.

Military Service Genealogy Searches can be conducted at the General Reference Branch, National Archives and Records Administration, Washington, DC 20408, (202) 501-5430. This office maintains military service and pension records of people who served prior to 1900. The office accepts written requests only. Ask for Form NATF 80. If information is found, a small fee will be charged and appropriate military documents will be released.

Prisoner-of-War Records can be found at:

Military Services Branch
National Archives and Records Administration
Eighth St. and Pennsylvania Ave., NW, Room 13W
Washington, DC 20408
(202) 501-5385

This office has information regarding current Prisoner-of-War records through the Civil War, and can also direct you to the proper office for information regarding prisoners-of-war to the present.

The Center for Electronic Records, National Archives and Records Administration, Washington, DC 20408, (202) 501-5400, holds all Federal records on computer disk, which include all recent Department of Defense records and the casualty lists from the Vietnam War. Copies may be purchased.

REGIONAL ARCHIVES SYSTEM QUICKLIST

The following list contains for each regional archive, name, mailing address, phone number, fax number, Internet address, hours, and areas from which it acquires and maintains permanent, non-current Federal records.

National Archives—New England Region
380 Trapelo Road
Waltham, Massachusetts 02154-6399
Phone: 617-647-8100 / Fax: 617-647-8460
Internet: archives@waltham.nara.gov
Connecticut, Maine, Massachusetts, New Hampshire, Rhode Island, and Vermont

National Archives—Pittsfield Region
100 Dan Fox Drive
Pittsfield, Massachusetts 01201-8230
Phone: 413-445-6885 / Fax: 413-445-7599
Internet: archives@pittsfield.nara.gov
Microfilm only

National Archives—Northeast Region
201 Varick Street
New York, New York 10014-4811
Phone: 212-337-1300 / Fax: 212-337-1306
Internet: archives@newyork.nara.gov
New Jersey, New York, Puerto Rico, and the U.S. Virgin Islands

National Archives—Mid-Atlantic Region
900 Market Street, Room 1350
Philadelphia, Pennsylvania 19107-4292
Phone: 215-597-3000 / Fax: 215-597-2303
Internet: archives@philarch.nara.gov
Delaware, Maryland, Pennsylvania, Virginia, and West Virginia

National Archives—Southeast Region
1557 St. Joseph Avenue
East Point, Georgia 30344-2593
Phone: 404-763-7477 / Fax: 404-763-7033
Internet: archives@atlanta.nara.gov
Alabama, Florida, Georgia, Kentucky, Mississippi, North Carolina, South Carolina, and
    Tennessee

National Archives—Great Lakes Region
7358 South Pulaski Road
Chicago, Illinois 60629-5898
Phone: 312-353-0162 / Fax: 312-353-1294
Internet: archives@chicago.nara.gov
Illinois, Indiana, Michigan, Minnesota, Ohio, and Wisconsin

National Archives—Central Plains Region
2312 East Bannister Road
Kansas City, Missouri 64131
Phone: 816-926-6272 / Fax: 816-926-6982
Internet: archives@kansascity.nara.gov
Iowa, Kansas, Missouri, and Nebraska

National Archives—Southwest Region
501 West Felix Street, Building 1
P.O. Box 6216
Fort Worth, Texas 76115-3405
Phone: 817-334-5525 / Fax: 817-334-5621
Internet: archives@ftworth.nara.gov
Arkansas, Louisiana, Oklahoma, and Texas

National Archives—Rocky Mountain Region
Denver Federal Center, Building 48
P.O. Box 25307
Denver, Colorado 80225-0307
Phone: 303-236-0817 / Fax: 303-236-9354
Internet: archives@denver.nara.gov
Colorado, Montana, New Mexico, North Dakota, South Dakota, Utah, and Wyoming

National Archives—Pacific Southwest Region
24000 Avila Road, 1st Floor East
P.O. Box 6719
Laguna Niguel, California 92607-6719
Phone: 714-360-2641 / Fax: 714-360-2644
Internet: archives@laguna.nara.gov
Hours: 8:00 A.M. to 4:30 P.M., Monday-Friday
8:00 A.M. to 4:00 P.M., first Saturday each month (Microfilm research only)
Arizona, Southern California, and Clark County, Nevada

National Archives—Pacific Sierra Region
1000 Commodore Drive
San Bruno, California 94066-2350
Phone: 415-876-9009 / Fax: 415-876-9233
Internet: archives@sanbruno.nara.gov
Northern California, Hawaii, Nevada (not Clark County), the Pacific Trust Territories, and
   American Samoa

National Archives—Pacific Northwest Region
6125 Sand Point Way NE
Seattle, Washington 98115-7433
Phone: 206-526-6507 / Fax: 206-526-4344
Internet: archives@seattle.nara.gov
Idaho, Oregon, and Washington

National Archives—Alaska Region
654 West Third Avenue
Anchorage, Alaska 99501-2145
Phone: 907-271-2441 / Fax: 907-271-2442
Internet: archives@alaska.nara.gov
Alaska

ADDITIONAL GENEALOGY AND CURRENT INFORMATION
FROM THE U.S. GOVERNMENT

The Biographical Directory of the U.S. Congress 1774-1989, contains authoritative bi-
ographies of the more than 11,000 men and women who have served in the U.S. Congress
from 1789 to 1989, and in the Continental Congress between 1774 and 1789. The latest
edition is published at the beginning of each Congress and is available through the Government Printing Office for a price from the Superintendent of Documents, Government
Printing Office, Washington, DC 20402, (202) 783-3238.

Some historical data on federal employees' personnel records are available and
transferred for storage in the National Personnel Records Center. The Center can provide
answers to questions regarding the information available and can provide copies of documents. Contact the Center for more information at the National Personnel Records Center, National Archives and Records Administration, 111 Winnebago Street, St. Louis, MO
63118, (314) 538-4261.

The Military and Civilian Employment Records, National Personnel Center, 9700
Page Blvd., St. Louis, MO 63232, (314) 538-5201/4261, holds both military and civilian
Federal personnel records dating from 1900 to the present. The Center prefers written requests for reference assistance. Full name and date of birth is needed. Costs available on
request.

The Data User Services Division, Bureau of the Census, U.S. Department of Commerce, Washington, DC 20233 (301) 763-7936, employs a Census History staff to search

the Federal censuses of population from seventy-two years ago and earlier for persons, and thirty years ago and earlier for businesses. Stored at Pittsburgh, Kansas, official transcripts of personal data can be provided to individuals, their representatives, or their survivors, requiring birth or citizenship documents. Government agencies and employers often accept these transcripts as evidence of age and place of birth for obtaining social security benefits, old age assistance, passports, naturalization papers, or delayed birth certificates, and for other purposes. The personal information recorded in these censuses may be furnished only upon the written request of the named individual or his or her legal representative. Application forms are needed for requests. Historical personal and business census data can generally be found on file at your local county and state Government archived libraries.

The Office of the Undersecretary of Defense, 400 Defense Pentagon, Room 3E764, Washington, DC 20301-4000, (703) 695-7402, has information on conscientious objectors and POWs, including reclassifications and discharge data.

Individual Selective Service registration status can be checked by calling or writing the Registration Information Office, P.O. Box 4638, North Suburban, IL 60197-4638, (708) 688-6888.

ADDITIONAL GENEALOGY FROM SOURCES OTHER THAN THE U.S. GOVERNMENT

Beginners in genealogy searches should do two things immediately: interview elderly or infirm relatives. The importance of talking to relatives while they are still with you and able to provide key information cannot be overemphasized.

Then you should gather and organize all the information you have from various sources. You may already have enough to induce you to get some genealogical software to help in organizing your information. Be sure to document all your sources. Organization allows you to develop an overview of what you have so that you can better direct your research.

A good step is probably to locate your local LDS (Latter Day Saints, Mormon) Family History Center (FHC). Millions of church and county records are available at these Centers. They come from many sources but mostly from individuals or from LDS missionaries. Locations are sited throughout the United States, and an extensive computer data bank has been established called Family Search. There is no fee to use these facilities, but copies of records are 10¢ each, computer printouts are 5¢ each, and microfiche copies are 25¢ each. Here is a complete list of LDS Family History Centers:

Alabama
Athens
P.O. Box 452
205-881-4461

Birmingham
2768 Altadena Road
Birmingham, AL 35243
205-967-7279

Huntsville
1804 Sparkman Dr.
205-721-0905

Mobile
5520 Ziegler Blvd.
205-344-601

Alaska
Anchorage
2501 Maplewood St.
907-277-8433

Fairbanks
1500 Cowles St.
907-456-1095

Juneau
5100 Glacier Highway
907-586-2525

Ketchikan
LDS Meetinghouse
907-225-3291

Soldotna
159 Marydale Dr.
907-262-4253

Wasilla
Delwood at Bogard Road
907-376-9774

Arizona
Cottonwood
127 Tenth St.
602-634-2349

Flagstaff
625 East Cherry
602-774-8576

Globe
Highway 60
602-425-9570

Holbrook
1600 North 2nd Avenue
602-524-6341

Kingman
3180 Rutherford Dr.
602-753-5144

Mesa
464 East First Ave.
602-964-2051

Page
313 Lake Powell Blvd.
602-645-2282

Peoria
12951 North 83rd Ave.
(no phone listed)

Phoenix
4601 West Encanto Blvd.
602-278-6863

Phoenix
8710 North 3rd Ave.
602-371-0649

Phoenix
3102 North 18th Ave.
602-265-7762

Phoenix
1315 East Cherry Lynn
601-231-9331

Prescott
1001 Ruth Street
602-778-2311

Safford
501 Catalina Dr.
602-428-3194

St. David
Main Street
602-586-4879

St. Johns
135 West Cleveland St.
602-337-2543

Show Low
West Highway 60
602-537-2331

Sierra Vista
Yaqui St.
602-378-3216

Snowflake
225 West Freeman Ave.
602-536-7430

Tucson
500 South Langley
602-298-0905

Winslow
Kingsley and Lee
602-289-5496

Yuma
4300 West 16th Street
602-782-6364

Arkansas
Fort Smith
(no address yet)
501-484-5304

Jacksonville
Highway 67 North
501-982-7967

Little Rock
13901 Quail Run Drive
501-455-0335

California
Anaheim
440 North Loara (rear)
714-635-2471

Anderson
4075 Riverside Avenue
916-365-8448

Bakersfield
316 A Street
805-325-8907

Barstow
2571 Barstow Road
714-252-4117

Blythe
3rd and Bernard
619-922-4019

Buena Park
7600 Crescent Avenue
714-828-1561

Camarillo
1201 Pasco
805-987-9232

Canyon Country
19513 Drycliff
805-251-5539

Carlsbad
1981 Chestnut Street
619-729-9770

Cerritos
17909 Bloomfield Avenue
213-924-3676

Cerritos—see Norwalk

Chatsworth
10123 Oakdale Avenue
(no phone listed)

Chico
2430 Mariposa Avenue
916-343-6641

Corona
1501 Taber Road
714-735-2619

Covina
656 South Grand Avenue
818-331-7117

El Centro
1280 South 8th Street
619-353-6645

Escondido
191 East Washington
619-741-8441

Eureka
2806 Dalber
707-425-7411

Fairfield
2700 Camrose Drive
707-425-2027

Fresno
5685 North Cedar
209-431-3759

Fresno
6641 East Butler
209-255-4208

Glendale
1130 East Wilson Avenue
818-241-8763

Goleta
478 Cambridge Drive
805-964-8044

Gridley
290 Spruce Street
916-846-3921

Hacienda Heights
16750 Colima Road
818-961-8765

Hemet
425 North Kirby Avenue
714-658-8104

Highland
7000 Central Avenue
714-862-9972

La Crescenta
4550 Raymond Avenue
818-957-0925

Lancaster
3150 West Avenue K Street
805-943-9927

Long Beach—See Los Alamitos

Los Alamitos
4142 Cerritos Avenue
714-821-6914

Los Angeles
Temple Visitor's Center
10741 Santa Monica Blvd.
213-474-9990

Menlo Park
1105 Valparaiso Parkway
415-325-9711

Mission Viejo
27976 Marguerite Parkway
714-364-2742

Modesto
731 El Vista Avenue
209-577-9830

Monterey Park
2316 Hillview Avenue
213-726-8145

Napa
2590 Tower
(no phone listed)

Needles
El Monte and Lilly Hill Drive
619-326-3363

Newbury Park
35 South Wendy Drive
619-326-3363

Norwalk
15311 South Pioneer Blvd.
213-868-8727

Oakland
4780 Lincoln Avenue
415-531-3905

Orange
674 Yorba Street
714-997-7710

Palmdale
2120 East Avenue "R"
805-947-1694

Palm Desert
72-960 Park View
619-340-6094

Palm Springs—See Palm Desert

Pasadena
770 North Sierra Madre Villa
213-351-8517

Quincy
Bellamy Lane
916-283-3112

Rancho Palos Verdes
5845 Crestridge
213-541-5644

Redding
3410 Chumcreek Road
916-222-4949

Ridgecrest
501 North Norma Street
619-375-8100

Riverside
5900 Grand Avenue
714-784-1918

Riverside
4375 Jackson Street
714-687-5542

Sacramento
2745 Eastern Avenue
916-487-2090

San Bernardino—See Highland
and Yucaipa

San Bruno
975 Sneath Lane
415-873-1928

San Diego
3705 10th Avenue
619-295-0882

San Jose
2175 Santiago Street
408-251-3962

San Luis Obispo
55 Casa Street
805-543-6328

Santa Barbara—See Goleta

Santa Clara
875 Quince Avenue
408-241-1449

Santa Maria
908 East Sierra Madre Avenue
805-928-4722

Santa Rosa
1725 Peterson Lane
707-525-0399

Seaside
1024 Noche Buena
408-394-1124

Simi Valley
3979 Township
805-581-2456

Sonora
19481 Hillside Drive
(no phone listed)

Stockton
820 West Brookside Road
209-951-7060

Ukiah
1337 South Dora Street
707-468-5746

Upland
785 North San Antonio
714-985-8821

Van Nuys
15555 Saticoy
(no phone listed)

Ventura
3501 Loma Vista Drive
805-643-5607

Victorville
12100 Ridgecrest Road
619-243-5632

Visalia
825 West Tulare Avenue
209-732-3712

Watsonville
255 Holm
(no phone listed)

Westminister
10332 Bolsa
714-554-0592

Whittier
7906 South Pickering
213-693-5472

Yuba City
1470 Butte House Road
916-673-0113

Yucaipa
12776 6th Street
(no phone listed)

Colorado
Arvada
7080 Independence
303-421-0920

Boulder
701 West South Boulder Rd.
303-665-4685

Colorado Springs
1054 East Lasalle
303-634-0572

Cortez
1800 East Empire Street
303-565-4372

Craig
11th Finley
(no phone listed)

Denver (See also Arvada)
2710 South Monaco Parkway
303-756-6864

Durango
2nd Hill Top Circle
303-259-1061

Ft. Collins
600 East Swallow Drive
303-226-5999

Grand Junction
543 Melody Lane
303-243-2782

Greely
2207 23rd Avenue
303-352-2689

La Jara
718 Broadway
303-274-4032

Littleton (Columbine)
6705 East Easter Avenue
303-798-6461

Manassa—See La Jara

Meeker—See Craig

Montrose
Hillcrest and Stratford
303-249-4739

Northglen
100 East Malley Drive
303-451-7177

Pueblo
4720 Surfwood
303-564-0793

Connecticut
Bloomfield
1000 Mountain Road
203-242-1607

Hartford—See Bloomfield

Madison
275 Warpas
203-245-4986

New Canaan
682 South Avenue
203-245-1305

Trumbull
39 Bonnie View
203-374-7444

Waterford
12 Dunbar Road
203-442-6644

Delaware
Wilmington
1443 Dickinson Lane
302-654-1911

Florida
Boca Raton
1530 West Camino Real
305-395-6644

Fort Myers
3105 Broadway
813-936-9831

Gainesville
3745 NW 16th Blvd.
904-377-9711

Homestead
29600 SW 167th Ave.
305-246-2486

Jacksonville
4087 Hendricks Ave.
904-398-3487

Lake Mary
Lake Emma Drive and Greenway Blvd.
305-321-7837

Marianna
1802 College Street
904-482-8159

Orange Park
461 Blanding Blvd.
904-272-1150

Orlando
45 East Par Ave.
305-898-3841

Panama City
3140 State Avenue
904-785-3601

Pensacola
5773 North 9th Avenue
904-476-0183

Plantation
851 North Hiatus Road
(no phone listed)

Rockledge
1801 Fisk Blvd.
305-636-2431

St. Petersburg
570 62nd Avenue North
813-525-9351

Tallahassee
312 Stadium Drive
904-224-6431

Tampa
4106 East Fletcher Ave.
813-971-2869

Winter Haven
2337 South Crystal Lake Drive
813-665-8707

Georgia
Augusta
2108 Eastland Drive
404-733-4773

Columbus
Reese Road
(no phone listed)

Dunwoody
1155 Mount Vernon Highway
404-393-4329

Macon
1624 Williamson Road
912-788-1293

Marietta
New Macland Road
(no phone listed)

Savannah
1234 King George Blvd.
912-927-6543

Valdosta
1307 West Alden Avenue
912-242-2300

Hawaii
Hilo
1373 Kilauea Avenue
808-935-0711

Honolulu
1500 South Beretania Street
808-941-1891

Honolulu
1723 Beckley St.
808-841-4118

Kaneohe
46-117 Halaulani St.
808-247-3134

Kona
Kalani Road
808-329-5054

Laie
55-600 Naniloa Loop
808-293-2133

Lihue
4598 East Hiku St.
(no phone listed)

Mililani
95-186 Wainaku Place
(no phone listed)

Idaho
Arco
Country Road
208-527-8900

Blackfoot
Old Seminary Bldg.
Route 3
208-785-5022

Blackfoot
101 North 900 West
208-684-3784

Boise
325 West State Street
208-334-2305

Boise (Meridian)
12040 West Amity Road
208-362-5847

Burley
224 East 14th Street
208-678-7286

Caldwell
3015 South Kimball
208-459-2531

Coeur d'Alene
2801 North 4th
208-765-0150

Driggs
221 North 1st East
208-354-2253

Emmett
980 West Central Road
208-365-4112

Firth
East Center Street
208-346-6282

Idaho Falls
1155 1st Street
208-524-5291

Idaho Falls
3000 Central Avenue
208-529-4087

Idaho Falls
1860 Kearny
208-529-9805

Idaho Falls
1450 Mt. View Lane
208-529-4974

Iona
Iona No. Road and US 26
(no phone listed)

Lewiston
9th & Preston
208-743-9744

Malad
20 South 100 West
208-766-2332

Meridian
Shamrock and McMillan Roads
208-376-0452

Montpelier
Bear Lake County Library
138 North 6th Street
208-847-0340

Nampa
143 Central Canyon
208-467-5827

Pocatello
156 1/2 South 6th Center
208-232-9262

Rexburg
Ricks College Library
208-356-2351

Salmon
400 South Daisy
208-756-3514

Sandpoint
433 South Boyer
208-263-8721

Shelly
325 East Locust
208-357-5505

Soda Springs
250 South 2nd East
208-547-3232

Twin Falls
401 Maurice Street North
208-733-8073

Weiser
306 East Main Street
208-549-1575

Illinois
Carbondale
Old Route 13
618-457-6994

Champaign
604 West Windsor Road
217-352-8063

Chicago Heights
402 Longwood Drive
312-754-2525

Fairview Heights
9827 Bunkum Road
(no phone listed)

Joilet
655 Springfield Avenue
(no phone listed)

Naperville
25 West 341 Ridgeland Road
312-357-0211

Nauvoo
Durphy St.
217-453-6347

Peoria
3700 West Reservoir Blvd.
309-682-4073

Rockford
620 North Alpine Road
815-399-5448

Schaumburg
1320 West Schaumburg Road
312-882-9889

Wilmette
2801 Lake Avenue
312-251-9818

Indiana
Bloomington
2411 East 2nd Street
812-333-0050

Evansville
812-423-9832

Ft. Wayne
5401 St. Joe Road
219-485-9581

Indianapolis
900 East Stop 11 Road
317-888-6002

Noblesville
777 Sunblest Boulevard
317-849-6086

New Albany
1534 Slate Run Road

South Bend
3050 Edison Road
219-233-6501

Terre Haute
1845 North Center
812-234-0269

Iowa
Ames
2524 Hoover
515-232-3434

Cedar Rapids
4300 Trailridge Road SE
319-363-9343

Davenport
4929 Wisconsin Avenue
319-386-7547

Sioux City
1201 West Clifton
712-255-9686

West Des Moines
3301 Ashworth Road
515-225-0416

Kansas
Dodge City
2506 6th Avenue
316-225-6540

Olathe
15915 West 143rd Street
913-829-1775

Topeka
3611 SW Jewell
913-266-7503

Wichita
7011 East 13th Street
316-683-2951

Louisiana
Alexandria
611 Versailles St.
318-448-1842

Baton Rouge
5686 Winbourne Ave.
504-357-8385

Monroe
909 North 33rd St.
318-387-3793

Metairie
5025 Cleveland Place
504-885-3936

Shreveport
200 Carroll St.
318-868-5169

Maine
Bangor
639 Grandview Avenue
207-942-1911

Cape Elizabeth
2 Ocean House Road
207-799-7018

Caribo
46 Hardin
(no phone listed)

Farmingdale
Hasson Street
207-582-6418

Maryland
Ellicott City
4100 St. Johns Lane
301-465-1642

Frederick
199 North Place
(no phone listed)

Kensington
10000 Stoneybrook Drive
301-587-0042

Lutherville
1400 Dulaney Valley Road
301-821-9880

Massachusetts
Foxboro
76 Main
617-543-5284

Weston
150 Brown Street
617-235-9892

Michigan
Ann Arbor
914 Hill Street
313-995-0211

Bloomfield Hills
425 North Woodward Avenue
313-647-5671

East Lansing
431 Saginaw Street
517-332-2932

Grand Blanc
4285 McCandlish Road
313-694-3343

Grand Rapids
2780 Leonard NE
616-949-3343

Kalamazoo
1112 North Drake Road
616-342-1906

Marquette
Cherry Creek Road
906-249-1511

Midland
11700 West Sugnet Road
517-631-1120

Westland
77575 North Hix Road
313-459-4570

Mississippi
Clinton
1301 Pinehaven Rd.
601-924-2537

Columbus
708 Airline Rd.
(no phone listed)

Gulfort
Klein Rd. at David
601-8322-0195

Hattiesburg
US 11 South
601-544-9238

Missouri
Columbia
904 Old Highway 63 South
314-443-2048

Frontenac
10445 Clayton Road
314-993-2328

Independence
705 West Walnut
816-461-0245

Joplin
22nd and Indiana
417-623-6508

Kansas City
8144 Holmes
816-444-3444

Liberty
1130 Clayview Drive
816-781-8295

Springfield
1357 South Ingram Mill Road
417-887-8229

Montana
Billings
2929 Belvedere Drive
406-656-8859

Billings
1000 Wicks Lane
406-259-3348

Bozeman
2915 Coulter Drive
406-586-3880

Butte
3400 East 4 Mile Road
406-494-9909

Great Falls
1401 9th Street NW
406-453-4280

Helena
1610 East 6th Avenue
406-443-0716

Kalispel
Buffalo Hill & Bountiful Drive
406-752-5446

Missoula
3201 Bancroft Street
406-543-6148

Stevensville
Eastside Highway &
Middle Burnt Fork Road
406-777-2489

Nebraska
Grand Island
212 West 22nd
308-382-9418

Lincoln
3100 Old Cheney Road
402-423-4561

Omaha
11027 Marth Street
402-393-7641

Nevada
Elko
1651 Collage Parkway
702-738-4565

Ely
900 Avenue East
702-289-2287

Fallon
750 West Richards St.
702-423-2094

Las Vegas
509 South Ninth St.
702-382-9695

Logandale
Highway 169
702-398-3594

Reno
Washoe Public Library
301 South Center
702-785-4530

Sparks
2955 North Rock Boulevard
702-359-5834

Winnemucca
111 West Mcarthur Avenue
702-623-4413

New Hampshire
Concord
90 Clinton Street
603-2224-3061

Nashua
110 Concord Street
603-880-7371

New Jersey
East Brunswick
303 Dunham's Corner Rd.
201-254-1480

Moorestown
Bridgeboro Rd
609-234-9639

Morristown
283 James St.
201-539-5362

New Mexico
Albuquerque
1100 Montano Road NW
505-345-0406

Albuquerque
5709 Haines Ave. SE
505-266-4867

Carlsbad
1200 West Church and
Oak Street
505-885-1368

Farmington
400 West Apache
505-325-5813

Gallup
601 Susan Avenue
(no phone listed)

Grants
1010 Bondad
(no phone listed)

Las Cruces
1015 Telshore Blvd.
505-522-2300

Santa Fe
410 Rodeo Road
(no phone listed)

Silver City
491 West 12th Street
505-388-5711

New York
Jamestown
851 Forest Ave.
716-487-0830

Loundonville
411 London Rd.
518-462-3687

New York
1775 Broadway
(no phone listed)

New York
251 West 57th Street
(no phone listed)

Pittsford
460 Kreag Rd.
716-248-9930

Plainview
160 Washington Ave.
516-433-0122

Syracuse
801 East Colvin St.
315-478-9484

Vestal
305 Murray Hill Road
607-798-7424

Williamsville
1424 Maple Rd.
716-688-9759

North Carolina
Charlotte
3020 Hilliard Drive
704-535-0238

Fayetteville
3200 Scotty Hill Road
919-864-2080

Goldsboro
1000 Eleventh Street
919-735-0633

Greensboro
3719 Pinetop Road
919-288-6539

Hickory
Highway 127 North
704-324-2823

Kingston
3006 Carey Road
919-522-4671

Raleigh
5100 Six Forks Road
919-781-1662

Skyland
US 25A (Sweeten Creek
Road and Rosseraggon)
704-684-6646

Wilmington
514 South College Road
919-395-4456

Winston-Salem
4780 Westchester Drive
704-731-7911

North Dakota
Bismarck
1500 Country West Road
701-235-2961

Fargo
2502 17th Avenue South
701-235-2961

Minot
2025 9th Street NW
701-838-4486

Ohio
Akron
735 North Revere Road
216-864-0203

Cincinnati
Cornell and Snider Roads
513-489-3036

Cincinnati
5505 Bosworth Place
513-531-5624

Columbus
3648 Lieb Street
614-451-0483

Dayton
1500 Shiloh Springs Road
513-854-4566

Fairbourn
3080 Bell Drive
513-878-9551

Kirtland
8751 Kirkland Road
216-256-8808

Reynoldsburg
2135 Baldwin Road
614-886-7686

Toledo
1545 East Gate
419-382-3498

Westlake
25000 Westwood Road
216-777-1518

Oklahoma
Lawton
923 Hilltop Drive
405-355-9946

Muskogee
3008 East Hancock Rd.
918-687-8861

Norman
Imhoff Rd. & Highway 9
405-364-8337

Oklahoma City
5020 NW 63rd
405-721-8455

Stillwater
1720 East Virginia
405-372-8569

Tulsa
12110 East 7th St.
918-437-5690

Oregon
Beaverton
4195 SW 99th
503-644-7782

Bend
1260 Thompson Dr.
503-389-3559

Central Point
2305 Taylor Rd.
503-664-5620

Coos Bay
3950 Sherman Ave.
503-269-9037

Corvallis
4141 NW Harrison
(no phone listed)

Eugene
3550 West 18th St.
503-343-3741

Grants Pass
1969 Williams Highway
503-479-7644

Gresham
3500 SE 182nd
503-665-1524

Hermiston
850 SW 11th
503-567-3445

Hillsboro
2200 NE Jackson School Rd.
503-640-4658

Klamath Falls
McClellan Drive at Alva
503-884-2133

La Grande
2504 North Fir
503-963-5003

Lake Oswego
1271 Overlook Drive
503-638-8486

McMinnville
1645 NW Baker
503-434-5681

Medford
2900 Juanipero Way
503-773-3363

Nyssa
West Alberta Ave.
503-372-5255

Ontario
1705 NW 4th Ave.
503-889-9350

Oregon City
14340 South Donovan Road
503-657-9584

Portland
2931 SE Harrison
503-235-9090

Pennsylvania
Broomall
721 Paxon Hollow Road
215-356-8507

Clark's Summit
Leach Hill &
Griffin Pond Roads
717-587-5123

Erie
1101 South Hill Road
814-866-3611

Knox
Clarion Road
814-797-1287

Philadelphia
See Broomall

Pittsburg
46 School Street
412-921-0235

Reading
3344 Reading Crest Ave.
215-929-0235

State College
842 Whitehall Road
814-238-4560

York
2100 Hollywood Drive
717-854-9331

Rhode Island
Providence
1000 Narragansett Parkway
401-463-9350

South Carolina
Charleston
1310 Sam Rittenburg
(Highway 7)
803-766-6017

Columbia
4440 Ft. Jackson Blvd.
803-782-7141

Florence
1620 Maldin Drive
803-662-9482

Greenville
Boiling Springs Road
803-234-5862

West Columbia
2108 Eastland Drive
404-733-4773

South Dakota
Rapid City
2822 Canyon Lane Drive
605-341-8572

Rosebud
L.D.S. Church
(no phone listed)

Sioux Falls
3900 South Fairhall Avenue
605-361-1070

Tennessee
Chattanooga
1019 North Moore Road
615-892-7632

Franklin
Corner of Spence Creek Road and Gray
    Fox Lane
(no phone listed)

Kingsport
100 Canongate Road
615-245-2321

Knoxville
400 Kendall Road
615-690-4041

Madison
107 Twin Hills Drive
615-859-6926

Memphis
8150 Walnut Grove Road
901-754-2545

Texas
Abilene
3325 North 12th St.
915-673-8836

Amarillo
5401 Bell St.
806-353-4796

Austin
1000 East Rutherford
512-837-3626

Bryan
1200 Barak Lane
409-846-7929

Corpus Christi
6750 Woodridge Rd.
512-993-2970

Dallas
10701 Lake Highlands Dr.
214-349-0730

Denton
1801 Malone
817-387-3065

Duncanville
1019 Big Stone Gap
214-709-0066

El Paso
3651 Douglas Ave.
915-565-9711

Fort Worth
5001 Altamesa Blvd.
817-292-8393

Friendswood
505 Deseret
713-996-9346

Harlingen
2320 Haine Dr.
(no phone listed)

Houston
10555 Mills Road
713-890-7434

Houston
1101 Bering Dr.
713-785-2105

Houston
4202 Yellowstone
713-487-1409

Houston
16331 Hafer Rd.
713-893-5381

Killeen
1410 South 2nd St.
817-526-2918

Kingwood
4021 Deerbrook
713-360-1263

Longview
1700 Blueridge Parkway
214-759-7911

Lubbock
3211 58th St.
806-792-5040

McAllen
2nd Street La Vista
512-682-0051

Odessa
2011 North Washington
915-332-9221

Orange
6108 Hazelwood
(no phone listed)

Plano
2700 Roundrock
214-867-6479

Port Arthur
3939 Turtle Creek Drive
409-722-4659

Richland Hills
4401 NE Loop 820
817-284-4472

San Antonio
2103 St. Cloud
512-736-2940

Sugarland
602 Eldridge Road
713-240-1524

Utah
Altamont
Main Street
801-454-3522

Beaver
210 North Main
801-678-2024

Brigham City
10 South 4th East
801-723-5995

Castledale
Stake Center
801-748-2555

Cedar City
370 South 200 East
801-586-2296

Delta
52 North 100 West
801-865-3312

Duchesne
Stake Center
801-738-5371

Ferron
555 South 400 West
(no phone listed)

Fillmore
21 South 300 West
801-743-6219

Garland
131 East 1500 South
801-257-7015

Heber City
781 South 200 East
801-654-2760

Helper
150 Ridgerway
(no phone listed)

Hurricane
37 South 200 West
801-635-2174

Kanab
202 East 100 North
801-644-5973

Lehi
200 North Center Street
801-836-2651

Loa
20 South 100 West
801-836-2651

Logan
50 North Main
801-752-0541

Manti
295 South Main
801-835-9981

Moab
701 Locust Lane
801-259-5563

Monticello
165 South Main
801-587-2607

Moroni
300 Orth Center St.
801-436-4497

Mount Pleasant
295 South State
(no phone listed)

Nephi
351 North 100 West
801-623-1378

Ogden
539 24th St.
801-393-5248

Parowan
87 West Center St.
801-477-8077

Price
85 East Fourth North
801-637-2071

Provo
4386 HBL Library
Brigham Young University
801-378-6200

Richfield
91 South 200 West
801-896-8057

Roosevelt
447 East Lagoon St.
801-722-3794

St. George
58 East 775 South
801-673-4591

Sandy
1700 East 9639 South
(no phone listed)

Santaquin
90 South 200 East
801-754-3725

South Jordan
2450 West 10400 South
801-254-0121

Springville
350 North 400 East
(no phone listed)

Tropic
Ward Chapel
801-679-8693

Vernal
613 West 2nd St.
801-789-2618

Wellington
Stake Center
(no phone listed)

Wendover
269 B Street
801-665-2220

Vermont
Berlin
Hersey Road
802-299-0898

Virginia
Annandale
3900 Howard Street
703-256-5518

Charlottesville
Hydraulic Road
804-973-6607

Dale City
3000 Dale Blvd.
703-670-5977

Newport News
901 Denbigh Blvd.
804-874-2335

Oakton
2719 Hunter
703-281-1836

Richmond
5600 Monument Ave.
801-288-1834

Salem
6311 Wayburn Drive
703-366-6727

Virginia Beach
4760 Princess Anne Rd.
804-467-3302

Waynesboro—See Charlottesville

Washington
Bellevue
10675 NE 20th St.
206-454-2690

Bremerton
2225 Perry Ave.
206-479-9370

Centralia
2801 Mount Vista Rd.
206-736-8476

Edmonds
7309 228th SW
206-774-0933

Elma
702 East Main
206-482-5982

Everett
9509 19th Ave. SE
206-337-0457

Federal Way
34815 32nd Ave. S
206-874-3803

Fennewick
515 South Union
(no phone listed)

Ferndale
5800 Northwest Ave.
206-384-6188

Lake Stevens
131 101st Ave. SE
206-335-0754

Longview
1721 30th Ave.
206-425-8409

Moses Lake
925 North Grape Dr.
509-765-8711

Mount Vernon
18th and Hazel
(no phone listed)

North Bend
527 Mount Si Blvd.
(no phone listed)

Olympia
1116 Yew St.
206-943-7055

Othello
12th and Rainer
509-488-6437

Pasco
2108 Road 24
509-545-4022

Pullman
NE 1055 Orchard Dr.
(no phone listed)

Quincy
1102 Second Ave. SE
(no phone listed)

Richland
1314 Goethals
509-946-6637

Seattle
142nd SW and Ambaum
Blvd. SW
206-246-7864

Seattle
5701 8th NE
206-522-1233

Silverdale
Nels Nelson Rd.
(no phone listed)

Spokane
North 919 Pines Road
509-926-0551

Sumner
512 Valley Ave.
206-863-3383

Tacoma
South 12th and Pearl St.
206-564-1103

Vancover
10509 SE 5th St.
206-256-7235

Walla Walla
1821 South 2nd St.
509-525-1121

Wenatchee
667 Tenth NE
509-884-3285

Yakima
705 South 38th Ave.
509-966-8510

West Virginia
Fairmont
Route 73 North
304-363-0116

Huntington
5640 Shawnee Drive
304-736-9072

Wisconsin
Eau Claire
3335 Stein Boulevard
715-834-8271

Hales Corner
9600 West Grange Avenue
414-425-4182

Madison
1711 University Avenue
608-238-1071

Shawano
910 East Zingler
715-526-2946

Wyoming
Afton
347 Jefferson
307-886-3905

Casper
Corner of Fox & 45th
307-234-3326

Cheyenne
Wyoming County Library
2800 Central Avenue
307-643-3561

Cody
1407 Heart Mountain
307-587-3427

Evanston
1224 Morse Lee Street
(no phone listed)

Gillette
1500 O'Hara
307-686-2077

Green River
120 Shoshone Avenue
307-875-3972

Jackson Hole
520 East Broadway
307-733-6337

Kemmerer
Antelope 3rd West Avenue
307-877-6502

Laramie
1219 Grand Avenue
(no phone listed)

Lovell
50 West Main
307-548-2963

Rawlings
117 West Kendrick Street
307-324-5459

Riverton
North 4th West and Elizabeth Drive
307-332-3666

Rock Springs
2055 Edgar Street
307-362-8062

Sheridan
2051 Colonial Drive
307-674-9904

Urie
Stake Center
307-786-4559

Worland
500 Sagebrush Drive
307-347-8958

Chapter 8

Information Brokers

You as the customer should receive satisfactory service. I thoroughly believe that clients of an information broker should demand quality service. For this reason, I have suggested only a few of the most noted. I have not worked with all of those on the list of information brokers below, but I have included them so you can check them out for yourself. These guidelines "should" include:

1. The broker should be in business five years or more. This can sometimes be waived if the company is duly licensed by the state in which they conduct business. For example, a licensed private investigator in California is checked out on criminal files, tested, and answerable to the State of California's Consumer Affairs Department.
2. The broker should have a professional private investigator's license or be a member of the Information Industry Association (IIP) or the Association Independent Information Providers (AIIP).
3. A responsible firm will also check you out, that is, verify that you are in business. A company that does this as a matter of policy is well managed and responsible and will be likely to do what they say.

I believe in quality in this business and will not recommend anyone that does not meet the few simple guidelines found above.

The oldest association of information specialists is the Information Industry Association (IIA), at 1625 Massachusetts Avenue, N.W., Suite 700, Washington, DC 20036, (202) 986-0280, and on the Internet at http://www.infoindustry.org. This includes a distinguished membership, including The American Stock Exchange, Barron's, America Online, and so on. This organization works closely with the U.S. Government in support of industry interests and is considered the most prestigious of the information associations.

I also like the Association of Independent Information Professionals (AIIP). Its code of ethics is outstanding. You can find out more about this organization and its code of ethics at 234 West Delaware Avenue, Pennington, NJ 08534, (609) 730-8759 and on the Internet at http://www.aiip.org. Begun in 1987, this organization now claims over 800 members. The organization provides an exchange of information to medium and small companies within the information industry.

LIST OF INFORMATION BROKERS

A Matter of Fact
2976 Camargo Ct.
San Jose, CA 95132
(408) 926-2125

Access Information Services
1323 26th Avenue
San Francisco, CA 94122
(415) 564-9096

Alex Kramer
1757 Lamont Street, NW
Washington, DC 20010
(202) 234-5410

Automated Data Retrieval Services
8934 Lakewood Drive, Suite 274
Windsor, CA 95492
(800) 270-2377

Ayers Information Network
3545 Indian Queen Lane
Philadelphia, PA 19129-1539
(215) 842-9450

Background America
1900 Church Street #400
Nashville, TN 37203
(800) 697-7189
http://www.background-us.com

Berinstein Research
5070 Campo Road
Woodland Hills, CA 91364
(818) 704-6460

Burana Consulting and Research
P.O. Box 1752
Lake Arrowhead, CA 92352
(909) 337-1484

Burwell Enterprises
3724 F.M. 1960 West, Suite 214
Houston, TX 77068
(713) 537-9051

Cal Info
1957 N. Bronson #101
Los Angeles, CA 90068
(213) 957-5035

CARCO Group Inc.
17 Flowerfield Industrial Park
St. James, NY 11780
(516) 584-7094

CDB InfoTek
6 Hutton Centre
Santa Ana, CA 92707
(800) 427-3747

CCH Incorporated
2700 Lake Cook Road
Riverwoods, IL 60015
(847) 267-7000

CK Research Associates
7570 Skillman #112
Dallas, TX 75231
(214) 503-7305

Chemcomm Corporation
P.O. Box 11206
Alexandria, VA 22312
(703) 998-4566

Clark Boardman Callaghan
375 Hudson Street
New York, NY 10014
(212) 924-7500

Competitive Analysis Technologies
11702-B Grant, Suite 112
Cypress, TX 77429
(713) 370-3846

Compton Research Services
P.O. Box 15895
Rio Rancho, NM 87174
(505) 899-2975

Continental Commercial Advisors
522 25th Street
Santa Monica, CA 90402
(310) 395-7027

Cooper Hydock Rugge, Inc.
622 S. 42nd Street
Philadelphia, PA 19104
(215) 823-5490

Cooper Information
5 Ellery Place
Cambridge, MA 02138
(617) 354-3274

Computer Assisted Research On Line
1166 N.E. 182nd Street
Miami, FL 33162
(800) 329-6397

Confi-chek Investigations
1507 24th Street
Sacramento, CA 95816
(800) 821-7404

C.V.P. Services
13613 Country Lane
Burnsville, MN 55337
(612) 435-7986

DAC Services
(800) 331-9175
http://www.dacservices.com

Deward Houck & Associates
P.O. Box 1185
Lakeside, CA 92040
(619) 390-7291

Dun & Bradstreet Information Services
3 Sylvan Way
Parsippany, NJ 07054
(800) 234-3867
Fax: (512) 794-7670
http://www.dbisna.com/

Fact or Fiction Research
240 South Grand Oaks Ave.
Pasadena, CA 91107
(818) 577-9311

FINDS/SVP, Inc.
625 Avenue of the Americas
New York, NY 10011
(212) 645-4500

Financial Investigative Services, Ltd.
P.O. Box 301
Augusta, ME 04332
(207) 622-5674

Fourth Wave, Inc.
P.O. Box 6547
Alexandria, VA 22306
(703) 360-4800

Franklin Information Group
4120 West Maplecrest Drive
Franklin, WI 53132
(414) 761-8771

FYI/Services
Box 84 Wittenberg Road
Bearsville, NY 12409
(914) 679-4815

Golden Information Group
753 N. 35ᵗʰ Street, Suite 312
Seattle, WA 98103
(206) 547-5662

Honolulu Information Service
P. O. Box 10447
Honolulu, HI 96816
(808) 733-2058

Infocite
8300 Chamberlin
Dexter, MI 48130-9327
(313) 426-4456

Information Edge
P.O. Box 373229
Satellite Beach, FL 32937
(407) 779-9161

Information Factory
Bayside 1001 Alternate A1A
Jupiter, FL 33477
(407) 622-1949

Information Matters
148 Hazel Drive
New Orleans, LA 70123
(504) 738-0070

Information Research Center
103 Five Oaks
San Antonio, TX 78209
(210) 829-0001

InfoSmith Research Services
107 S. Mary Ave., Suite 98
Sunnyvale, CA 94086
(408) 736-1107

Infotech Information & Research
11282 Washington Blvd.
Culver City, CA 90230
(310) 398-2568

InfoWorks
2033 Clement Ave., Suite 222
Alameda, CA 94501-1317
(510) 865-8087

Intelligence Network, Inc.
P.O. Box 727
Clearwater, FL 34617
(800) 562-4007

International Research Center
P.O. Box 825
Tempe, AZ 85281
(602) 470-0389

1FM Data Services
951-2 Old Country Rd., Suite 311
Belmont, CA 94002
(415) 570-5742

IQ Data
1401 El Camino, Suite 220
Sacramento, CA 98515
(800) 264-6517
http://www.iqdata.com (direct on-line
    access)

I.R.I.S.
2859 Galahad Drive NE
Atlanta, GA 30345-9459
(404) 321-9459

IRSC, Inc.
3777 N. Harbor Boulevard
Fullerton, California 92835
(800) 640-4772
Fax: (714) 738-9106
http://www.irsc.com

JAL Data Research Service
1110 Capitol Way South
Olympia, WA 98501
(360) 357-7040
(one product is Name Shark II)

Krauss Research
6114 LaSalle Ave., Suite 413
Oakland, CA 94611
(510) 482-8760

Knowledge Access International
2685 Marine Way, Suite 1305
Mountain View, CA 94043
(415) 969-0606

Law Library Management, Inc.
38 Bunker Hill Drive
Huntington, NY 11743
(516) 266-1093

Lawquest, Inc.
P.O. Box 342
Fanwood, NJ 07023
(908) 322-8489

LegalEase Inc.
139 Fulton Street, #1013
New York, NY 10038
(212) 393-9070

Lexis-Nexus
9393 Springboro Pike
P.O. Box 933
Dayton, Ohio 45401
(800) 227-9597

Library Specialists Inc.
1000 Johnson Ferry Rd., Suite G1000
Marietta, GA 30068
(770) 578-6200

Longheed Resource Group, Inc.
2704 Rew Circle, Suite 102
Ocoee, FL 34761
(407) 654-1212

McBride and Associate, PI
1124 2nd Street
Old Sacramento, CA 95814
(800) 995-9443
(a favorite of former law enforcement officers)

McComb Enterprises, Inc.
4144 W. Lake Road
Canandaigua, NY 14424
(716) 394-7350

Multi/Data Briefing Service
P.O. Box 94444
Birmingham, AL 35220-4444
(205) 856-1101

NorthWest Online
2817 East Main Avenue
Puyallup, WA 98372
(206) 848-7767
www.nwlocation.com

OPEN (Ohio Professional Electronic Network)
1650 Lake Shore Drive, Suite 180
Colombus, OH 43204
(614) 481-6999

Online Resources, Inc.
200 Little Falls St., #G-201
Falls Church, VA 22046
(800) 678-9393

Pallorium, Inc.
P.O. Box 155—Midwood Station
Brooklyn, NY 11230
(212) 969-0286

PFC Information Services
6114 La Salle Ave., #149
Oakland, CA 94611
(510) 653-0666

Pinkerton Services Group
6100 Fairview Rd, Suite 900
Charlotte, NC 27210
(800) 582-5745
www.worklife.com/pinkertn.htm

Research Data Service
9030 West Sahara Avenue #270
The Lakes, NV 89117
(702) 733-4990

Saporito & Associates
101 Murray Street
New York, NY 10007-2132
(212) 693-3474

Search International, Inc.
1870 N. Roselle Rd., Suite 105
Schaumburg, IL 60195
(708) 885-1950

Silver Birch Enterprises
1310 Maple Ave., Suite 3C
Evanston, IL 60201-4325
(708) 864-4494

Snoop With The Scoop
P.O. Box 32790
San Jose, CA 95152-2770
(408) 258-1272

Steven Youmans & Associates
P.O. Box 6704
Ventura, CA 93006-6704
(213) 489-2208

Sullivan & Associates
182 Oleander Drive
San Rafael, CA 94903
(415) 472-2145

TechnoSearch Inc.
3915 Mission Ave., #7-109
Oceanside, CA 92054
(619) 721-5500

Trans Union
1390 Willow Pass Road, Suite 620
Concord, CA 94520
(510) 689-1912 or (800) 899-7132
(They sell credit headers.)

TRW REDI Property Data
844 Folsom St. #207
San Francisco, CA 94107-1123
(415) 543-6710

Vista Information Solutions, Inc.
55 Madison Ave.
Morristown, NJ 07960-7397
(201) 984-0666

Chapter 9

Ethics and Final Thoughts

Locating people is a double-edged sword. On the one hand, reuniting missing family members or friends, or finding a guy that has skipped out on a loan, represents the upside. Happy times for the holidays is what we all envision from a successful union of family members, missing or unknown to the family. I take great satisfaction in the student who wrote that she had found a daughter she had not seen for forty years. She was even happier when she had discovered that she also had a son-in-law she had never meet. And as if this were not enough, this woman had two grandchildren. Being alone, she could not say enough about how much this reunion had meant to her. This is the image we all seek from a missing persons case.

The downside is the misuse of information—as in the tragic case of a young actress and the star of the television show *My Sister Sam*, Rebecca Schaffer, who was murdered by an obsessed fan. In this case, the irresponsible dissemination of private information led to disaster. Our industry was blamed, and rightfully so, by the Academy of Motion Pictures and by society in general. Other examples of the abuse of information are represented by the irresponsible use of the Internet and by the mistakes made by large companies and individuals alike. The Internet's exposure of individual social security numbers and drivers' records has brought close scrutiny of the industry by Federal agencies, the Congress, and the White House. Some information simply does not need to be disseminated in public forums. The danger here is that legitimate-use access to this information will become heavily regulated if a lid is not placed on the irresponsible disclosure of information. Of course, the responsibility must rest on the investigative and information professionals themselves. Each case must be scrutinized, for valid reasons, prior to the access of these powerful systems.

Businesses need access to some of this information for commerce. Without it, our fast-paced information, banking, and credit approval systems become slow-moving machines. There is nothing wrong with someone checking out the background of employees or babysitters. But each case must be examined on its merits, prior to an investigation or information being disseminated. The concept I suggest as our guide is called *ethos*.

Ethos is defined as self-regulating, guiding beliefs and commitments to standards of a group or community, a moral attitude or character. Using these powerful information systems for less than reasonable and legal reasons simply does not create the type of society most of us want, and it starts with each one of us. There is no middle ground here. Failure to apply ethical community standards to the dissemination of this information could lead to a severe limitation on information for everyone, including business. The last thing we want is criminals using these systems to hide and not be held accountable for their illegal acts. The highly respected pioneer in this field, Jack Reed, once said to me, "absolute privacy is anarchy."

I agree with Jack. I believe that businesses should have access to this type of information. But with access comes the imperative for responsible conduct and protection of this information. I never take a case without checking out a potential client's story. Most often I work for attorneys who have legitimate reasons for needing this information. These reports will help them in the normal conduct of the business of the legal community. Attorneys are Officers of the Court, duly sworn and licensed by the Bar Association, and they regularly need this information in the normal conduct of the business of the courts. Businesses also have a legitimate need for such information in conducting credit checks, assessing merger or acquisition opportunities, accounting for assets in post-judgment proceedings, and so on. However, I will never take on a client I have any reason to believe has devious or illegal intentions. Nor will I release information on the location of a person I have found before confirming that they are willing to approve this release. This is part and parcel of appropriate behavior in this business, and I can say that the overwhelming majority of professionals that I know abide meticulously by this code of conduct.

With that said, it is now time to take up your search. I wish you the very best of luck.

Index